James Floyd Kelly

D1470228

Sams **Teach Yourself**

Galaxy Tab™

in **10 Minutes**

SAMS | 800 East 96th Street, Indianapolis, Indiana 46240

Sams Teach Yourself Samsung Galaxy Tab™ in 10 Minutes
Copyright © 2011 by Pearson Education, Inc.

ISBN-13: 978-0-672-33682-9

ISBN-10: 0-672-33682-0

Library of Congress Cataloging-in-Publication data is on file.

Printed in the United States of America

First Printing: March 2011

Trademarks

All terms mentioned in this book that are known to be trademarks or service marks have been appropriately capitalized. Pearson cannot attest to the accuracy of this information. Use of a term in this book should not be regarded as affecting the validity of any trademark or service mark.

Warning and Disclaimer

Every effort has been made to make this book as complete and as accurate as possible, but no warranty or fitness is implied. The information provided is on an "as is" basis. The author and the publisher shall have neither liability nor responsibility to any person or entity with respect to any loss or damages arising from the information contained in this book.

Bulk Sales

Pearson offers excellent discounts on this book when ordered in quantity for bulk purchases or special sales. For more information, please contact

U.S. Corporate and Government Sales
1-800-382-3419
corpsales@pearsontechgroup.com

For sales outside of the U.S., please contact

International Sales
international@pearsoned.com

Editor in Chief
Greg Wiegand

Acquisitions Editor
Laura Norman

Development Editor
Wordsmithery LLC

Technical Editor
David Levy

Managing Editor
Sandra Schroeder

Project Editor
Seth Kerney

Copy Editor
Keith Cline

Indexer
Heather McNeill

Compositor
Mark Shirar

Book Designer
Gary Adair

Contents

About the Author

James Floyd Kelly received an English degree from the University of West Florida and an industrial engineering degree from Florida State University, and has enjoyed using the skills and knowledge from both in various jobs over the years.

He is the author of numerous books, including books on building a CNC machine, building and programming LEGO robotics, and using open source software.

He currently lives with his wife and two sons in Atlanta, Georgia.

Dedication

For Ashley. Thank you for nonstop encouragement and support.

Acknowledgments

I enjoyed writing this book, and my Pearson team made it that much more enjoyable. Special thanks to Laura Norman, for giving me a chance to write for Pearson and having much patience as I learned the ins and outs of the Pearson writing process and special software.

The rest of my team, whose names you can find a few pages back, were so helpful in getting this book done, and I'm indebted to Romny and Seth for helping pull it all together.

A special thank you to my tech editor and good friend, David Levy, who agreed to purchase a Galaxy Tab and help me out as my tech editor. His error-catching and suggestions for improving the book were invaluable.

Finally, I want to thank Yvonne Hargrove, for her persistence in helping me procure my Galaxy Tab, and Maris Whetstone, for some technical assistance and testing along the way.

We Want to Hear from You

As the reader of this book, you are our most important critic and commentator. We value your opinion and want to know what we're doing right, what we could do better, what areas you'd like to see us publish in, and any other words of wisdom you're willing to pass our way.

You can email or write me directly to let me know what you did or didn't like about this book—as well as what we can do to make our books stronger.

Please note that I cannot help you with technical problems related to the topic of this book, and that due to the high volume of mail I receive, I might not be able to reply to every message.

When you write, please be sure to include this book's title and author, as well as your name and contact information. I will carefully review your comments and share them with the author and editors who worked on the book.

Email: feedback@samspublishing.com

Mail: Greg Wiegand
          Editor in Chief
          Sams Publishing
          201 West 103rd Street
          Indianapolis, IN 46290 USA

Reader Services

Visit our website and register this book at informit.com/register for convenient access to any updates, downloads, or errata that might be available for this book.

Introduction

The Galaxy Tab hit the market with a bang! It's the first 7-inch tablet to become available with the Android operating system (and a 10-inch version is just on the horizon), a popular open source OS that is extremely versatile, stable, and feature packed. Add in the ability for third-party software developers to create new programs (called apps) for consumers, and the Galaxy Tab offers users a wide range of services, games, and capabilities in a portable and lightweight package.

Now, tablet computing is certainly not new—they started appearing in the mid-'90s and typically weighed as much as a laptop! The first attempt at tablets were nothing more than stripped-down laptops with hardware that really wasn't up to the task of running bloated operating systems and gargantuan programs that took forever to open and use. Tablets appeared and disappeared as consumers made their frustrations known, and sales plummeted.

Jump forward a decade and the day of the tablet has come again... but this time the technology appears to have matured. The Galaxy Tab is one of the newest tablets to hit the market, and it brings with it numerous hardware and software features that are sure to impress consumers—and maybe impress you. Whether you already own a Galaxy Tab or are considering purchasing one, this book provides you with information about the device's features and capabilities.

This book is all about getting a Galaxy Tab owner up to speed on using the Galaxy Tab and its most popular features. Lessons are short and quick—readers can get through a lesson in fewer than 10 minutes and then immediately put that new knowledge to work with a Galaxy Tab. The 10 lessons I cover in this book are as follows:

- ▶ Set up your Galaxy Tab using the Setup Wizard

- ▶ Customize your Galaxy Tab using the Settings tool

- ▶ Take photos and videos with the Camera app

- ► Browse the Internet and check email

- ► Navigate using GPS

- ► View photos and videos using the Gallery app

- ► Use the Android Market

- ► Video chat with the WebCam

- ► Take advantage of multimedia with eReader, Music, and YouTube

- ► Use custom apps and special features

Along with each lesson, I also provide tips and advice related to that lesson: shortcuts, faster methods, app recommendations, and more.

Who Is This Book For?

This book is for you if

- ► You are a new Galaxy Tab owner.

- ► You are considering purchasing a Galaxy Tab.

- ► You want more information on the built-in features of the Galaxy Tab.

- ► You're unfamiliar with how a particular app or hardware feature works.

- ► You want to learn about features on the Galaxy Tab not covered in the included user guide.

Conventions Used in This Book

I provide additional material in each lesson that might be useful to some
Galaxy Tab users but not everyone. This new information is provided in
the form of boxes, as described here:

> NOTE: A note presents interesting pieces of information related to
> the surrounding discussion.

> TIP: A tip offers advice or teaches an easier way to do something.

> CAUTION: A caution advises you about potential problems and
> helps you steer clear of disaster.

Screen Captures and Differences

Most of the figures in this book were taken directly from the Galaxy Tab
using its built-in screen-capture capability. However, there might be differ-
ences in what you see in a figure and what you see on your Galaxy Tab
screen. The Galaxy Tab is sold by numerous retailers, including electronics
stores and mobile phone companies. I purchased my Galaxy Tab, for
example, from Verizon Wireless.

Each company can customize the Galaxy Tab and load it with apps of its
own choosing. Some of these apps are trial apps—you can use them for a
few days or weeks and then must decide whether you want to purchase the
full app. Other apps provide access to specific services offered by a company—the screen shots in this book, for example, are taken from a Galaxy
Tab purchased from Verizon Wireless, and many of the apps you see in
screenshots are Verizon apps that add additional functionality to the
device. I don't cover apps that are specific to a certain retailer; instead, I
focus on those apps and features that are useful and available to all Galaxy
Tab owners, regardless of where they purchased their Galaxy Tab.

Finally, keep in mind that the Android operating system is an ever-evolving piece of software, and the OS and the many apps that run on Android are constantly being updated and improved. You might find some information in this book has changed for an app or for the Android OS if an update/upgrade has become available to the Galaxy Tab. A great place to search for information about updates to the Galaxy Tab's OS and apps is the Samsung website for the Galaxy Tab, found at http://www.samsung.com/us/mobile/galaxy-tab.

LESSON 1

The Setup Wizard

In this lesson, you learn how to use the Setup Wizard to configure many of the services and apps that you'll use with your Galaxy Tab. You also learn how to create a Google user account that is required for many services used on the Galaxy Tab.

Activate Your Galaxy Tab

The first time you turn on the Galaxy Tab, you are greeted with a screen that's locked. This is the default setting—if no action is taken within a few seconds, the device goes into Sleep mode and the screen turns off. To unlock the Galaxy Tab, put your finger on the **Unlock** button shown in Figure 1.1. Notice also in Figure 1.1 that the Galaxy Tab's control buttons (Menu, Home, Return, and Search) are also indicated.

The Unlock button: Tap and drag to the right.

FIGURE 1.1 Unlock the Galaxy Tab to gain access to the Setup Wizard.

You are next led through the Setup Wizard, which helps you configure various settings for your Galaxy Tab.

After unlocking the screen and starting the Setup Wizard, you are next asked to specify the language to use for the device. As you can see in Figure 1.2, my only choices were English and Spanish (Español). You might have additional language options available. Touch your finger on the language you want to use.

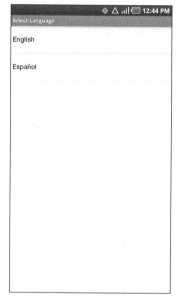

FIGURE 1.2   Choose a language for your Galaxy Tab.

In some instances, the carrier from which you purchased your Galaxy Tab might have already configured the language setting. If this is the case, feel free to jump ahead to Lesson 2, "Configuration and Notifications," or continue reading if you think there might be some settings that you want to change.

After selecting your language, you need to activate the Galaxy Tab. You see an alert screen such as the one in Figure 1.3. Tap the **Activate** button to begin the activation process.

As the activation process continues, you see a message like the one in Figure 1.4 that tells you the operating system is being set up. Be patient—this takes only a minute or so to complete.

FIGURE 1.3 Your Galaxy Tab must be activated before it can run.

FIGURE 1.4 The operating system program continues to install.

Connecting to a Network and Google Account

After your Galaxy Tab has activated, you are presented with a screen like the one in Figure 1.5. A Google user account is required for many of the Galaxy Tab features, including synchronization of your Gmail contacts and Google Calendar events.

At this point, either a Wi-Fi or 3G data connection must be made. If your Galaxy Tab is not connected (and it shouldn't be when you first activate) and a Wi-Fi network is not found or a 3G data connection has not been automatically made, a screen like the one shown in Figure 1.6 might pop up, asking you to connect to a Wi-Fi connection (with a password) or to enable 3G data connectivity. If you don't see this screen, your Galaxy Tab was able to make a Wi-Fi connection without a password. (This might occur at a Wi-Fi hotspot that does not require authentication.)

Tap the **Connect to Wi-Fi** button, and you are provided a list of Wi-Fi networks that are detected, as shown in Figure 1.7.

FIGURE 1.5   You must have a Google account before you can continue.

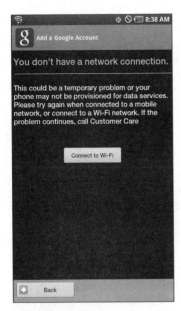

FIGURE 1.6 Wi-Fi or 3G data connectivity must be established.

FIGURE 1.7 Join a Wi-Fi network to continue with the Setup Wizard.

NOTE: **No Wi-Fi Networks Found**
Another option is to enable a connection with your mobile network. Because the instructions for doing this vary from carrier to carrier, contact your mobile carrier for details.

If your Galaxy Tab does not detect any Wi-Fi networks or you do not have the password to successfully connect to a Wi-Fi network, you need to stop and continue the Setup Wizard at a later time. You can cancel the Setup Wizard and run it later by tapping the **Home** button on the Galaxy Tab. Run the Setup Wizard again later by tapping the **Menu** button, selecting the **Settings** option, and then scrolling down the page and selecting the **Setup Wizard**, as shown in Figure 1.8.

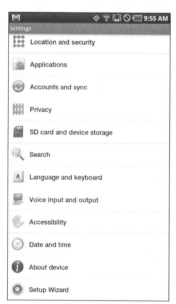

FIGURE 1.8   Run the Setup Wizard any time from the Settings screen.

If you are able to make a Wi-Fi or 3G data connection, the Setup Wizard continues by asking whether you already have a Google user account. If you do, tap the **Sign In** button as shown in Figure 1.9. Otherwise, tap the **Create** button.

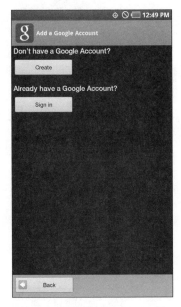

FIGURE 1.9   Log in to your Google account, or create one.

If you tap the **Sign In** button, you see a screen like the one in Figure 1.10. Simply enter in your Google username and password and tap the **Sign In** button. Tap the **Back** button to cancel the action and return to the previous screen.

If you click the **Create** button, you are guided through a short process to create a Google account. The first screen you see looks like Figure 1.11 and asks you to provide some basic details.

Tap the **Next** button and provide a password, as shown in Figure 1.12, and then tap the **Next** button again.

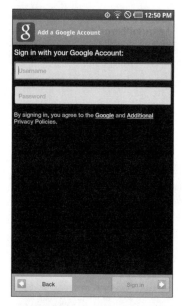

FIGURE 1.10   Log in to an existing Google account.

FIGURE 1.11   Create an account by providing your name and a username.

FIGURE 1.12   Give your Google account a strong password.

Now provide an answer to a security question (click the drop-down menu to choose from a variety of questions) and tap the **Create** button, as shown in Figure 1.13.

Next, read over the Google terms of service and tap the **I Agree, Next** button to accept the terms, as shown in Figure 1.14. (If you don't accept the terms, you cannot create a Google account and cannot use many Google services on your Galaxy Tab.)

Enter the letters you see in the box, as shown in Figure 1.15. This is a security step to verify that a human is creating the account and not a bot (an application written to automate tasks such as user account creation for spammers and other bad guys).

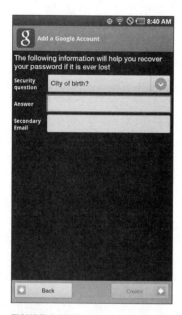

FIGURE 1.13   Answer a security question to finish the account-creation process.

FIGURE 1.14   Accept Google's terms of service.

FIGURE 1.15   Prove you're human by entering some text.

Synchronizing with Your Google Account

After you create your Google account, the Galaxy Tab next offers you the ability to synchronize your Google account, synchronizing your contacts, Calendar, and email (for your Gmail account that is automatically created for you when you create a Google user account) to the Galaxy Tab. Figure 1.16 shows the screen that enables you to do this. Tap the **Next** button to perform the synchronization (recommended) or uncheck the box at the bottom to disable the synchronization process.

This doesn't take long, and after the synchronization is done, you see a window like the one in Figure 1.17. Tap the **Finish** button to continue.

FIGURE 1.16   Syncing your data is recommended.

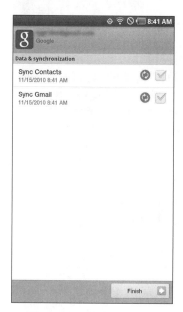

FIGURE 1.17   Select Contacts and/or Gmail to synchronize.

A confirmation screen appears, as shown in Figure 1.18, to let you know that your Google account has now been synced with the Galaxy Tab—from now on, you are able to access phone numbers, email addresses, and other contact information on your Galaxy Tab, even if a Wi-Fi or 3G data connection isn't present. Click the **Finish Setup** button to complete the account-creation and synchronization process.

FIGURE 1.18   You're told when the synchronization is completed.

Synchronizing with Other Services

The next screen you see looks like Figure 1.19. From this screen, you can configure other services such as Facebook, Yahoo! email, Twitter, and more.

Tap any of the icons to configure that service. If the service offers its own contact information (such as your Facebook friends' phone numbers, addresses, and more), you have a chance to synchronize these to your Galaxy Tab, as well.

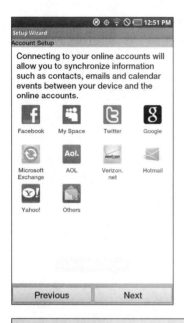

FIGURE 1.19 More services can be added and synced with your Galaxy Tab.

NOTE: **The Facebook App**

If you want to access your Facebook account, you either need to browse to the Facebook website or install a Facebook app (there are many)—see Lesson 7, "Shop the Android Market," for more information. This synchronization task only copies your Facebook contacts with the Galaxy Tab.

For example, following is an example of how to add a Facebook account to the Galaxy Tab. Just tap the **Facebook** icon in Figure 1.19 and you see a screen like the one shown in Figure 1.20.

After entering your username and password, tap the **Log In** button and specify how often Facebook data on the Galaxy Tab should be synchronized with your real Facebook account (see Figure 1.21).

After selecting a time period for synchronization, tap the **Next** button. You have the option to choose what information on Facebook is synchronized, as shown in Figure 1.22. Leave all the boxes checked to sync your Facebook friends' updates and pictures, sync your friends' contact information, and sync calendar information. Uncheck a box to disable the synchronization of that information.

FIGURE 1.20 Adding a Facebook account to the Galaxy Tab.

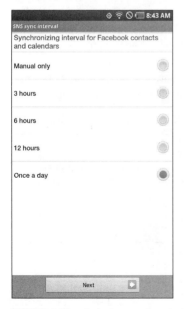

FIGURE 1.21 Select a synchronization time for the Facebook account.

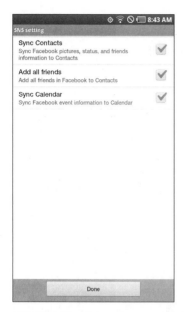

FIGURE 1.22   Select items to synchronize from the Facebook account.

Tap the **Done** button and... you're done! You can now view your Facebook contacts on your Galaxy Tab (using the Contacts app), even when a Wi-Fi or 3G connection isn't available. (If you want to view your actual Facebook page or your friends' pages, you need to install a Facebook app. See Lesson 7 for coverage of finding, downloading, and installing apps.)

TIP: **Configuring More Services**

To return to the screen shown in Figure 1.19, simply click the **Home** button on your Galaxy Tab and select **Settings**. Scroll down the list of settings and choose **Setup Wizard**. Tap the **Skip** button to skip setting up another Google account, and then you are taken to the setup screen to configure services such as Twitter, Myspace, and others.

Summary

In this lesson, you learned how to activate your Galaxy Tab, configure a Google account (or sign in with an existing one), and synchronize that account's data on the Galaxy Tab. You also learned how to add other services such as Facebook and how to configure them for synchronization.

Configuration and Notifications

In this lesson, you learn about the three ways to customize your Galaxy Tab, including configuring settings and notifications and customizing your screens.

Modifying Galaxy Tab Settings

The Settings tool contains the largest assortment of configuration options for your Galaxy Tab. Although you're unlikely to ever change many of these settings (such as the Language), you might find yourself modifying any number of them from time to time. I cannot cover every option in the Settings tool, but I show you how to access it and cover some of the settings that you are likely to need to change periodically.

First, you need to locate the Settings tool. To do this, you need to be viewing a home page, as shown in Figure 2.1. You swipe your finger left or right to view the various home pages, but you can access the Settings tool from any home page. Press the Home key, even if you are running an app, and you'll be taken to the home page.

Next, tap the **Menu** button on the Galaxy Tab. A small menu with six options appears: Add, Wallpaper, Search, Notifications, Edit, and Settings. You can see these options in Figure 2.2.

FIGURE 2.1   You access the Settings tool from any home page.

FIGURE 2.2   The Menu button offers six different options.

Tap the **Settings** option and the Settings tool appears, as shown in Figure
2.3. The Settings tool scrolls up and down the screen, so use your finger to
swipe the screen and scroll down to view all the options. In Figure 2.3,
only 12 options are visible, but 3 more options are available in the Settings
tool below the Accessibility option: Date and Time, About Device, and
Setup Wizard.

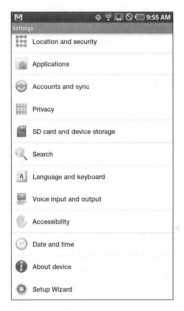

FIGURE 2.3   The Settings tool offers 15 options for configuration.

To select an option from the Settings tool, simply tap one of the options
with your finger, and you then are taken to a more detailed screen where
you can customize the selected option on your Galaxy Tab. Figure 2.4, for
example, shows the options available after the SD Card and Device
Storage option is selected.

In Figure 2.4, you can view the total space available on the memory card
and the amount of available space. You can also tap **Unmount SD Card**
when you want to remove it. For a quick erase, you can also tap **Format
SD Card**. And finally, the Galaxy Tab's available internal memory is also
displayed. Click the **Return** button to return to the Settings tool selections.

FIGURE 2.4   The SD card screen provides details and options related to the external SD memory card.

Now let's look at a few of the other Settings tools and see how they work. Tap the **Sound Settings** option, and you see a screen like the one in Figure 2.5.

If a box is grayed out (such as Silent mode in Figure 2.5), you can simply touch the box, and a green check mark appears in the box to indicate that feature is enabled. A right-pointing arrow such as the one shown to the right of the Vibrate selection tells you that there are multiple choices from which you can select. Tap the arrow and you can select an option from a pop-up window. Figure 2.6 shows the pop-up window that opens after you tap the **Vibrate** option.

Select an option (such as Always) or tap the **Cancel** button to leave the current configuration alone. Refer to Figure 2.5 to see that most setting options have a bit of text below the name of the option to let you know what the settings do. Audible Selection, for example, has the following description: Play sound when making screen selection. Remember that you can always undo a selection if you find that a configuration is annoying or doesn't work as you desire.

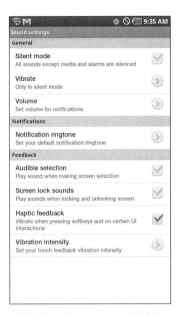

FIGURE 2.5   Configure sound settings such as Silent mode or Vibrate.

FIGURE 2.6   The Vibrate options offer four different selections.

Let's next look at the display settings shown in Figure 2.7. From here, you can control the screen's brightness, the font used for all display text, and color tweaks such as white and black color density and saturation.

FIGURE 2.7   Use display settings to tweak the LCD screen on your Galaxy Tab.

Two important settings that I want to point out in Figure 2.7 are the Power Saving Mode and the Screen Timeout. Click the **Screen Timeout** arrow to see the options shown in Figure 2.8. It gets a bit annoying to have the screen shut off after 15 or 30 seconds, so you might find setting it to 2, 10, or 30 minutes works best for you. More battery power is consumed while the LCD screen is lit, even if you're not using the Galaxy Tab, so the 1-hour selection is probably not a good choice for saving power.

The Power Saving mode is just a check box that is checked or unchecked. Placing a check in the box enables your Galaxy Tab to control the brightness of the screen based on your location's lighting level and other factors. It is recommended that you leave the box checked, but feel free to turn it off to test what kind of power consumption your Galaxy Tab experiences with the feature disabled.

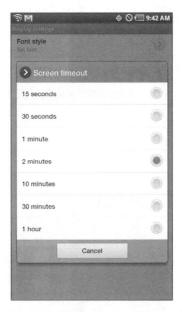

FIGURE 2.8   The Screen Timeout has seven options available.

There are 12 more Settings selections that you can experiment with, including wireless and network settings, privacy controls, and date and time configurations. I encourage you to go through each of the options available to see what settings can be turned on and off and what settings have options that can make using your Galaxy Tab more enjoyable and more efficient (for power and for ease of use).

Customizing Notifications

In addition to the Settings tool, your Galaxy Tab offers another way for you to customize your device: the Notifications tool. Refer to Figure 2.2 to see that the Notifications selection is on the pop-up menu that appears when you tap the Menu button. Tap **Notifications** to see a screen similar to the one shown in Figure 2.9.

Along the top of the screen you see five buttons: Wi-Fi, Bluetooth, GPS, Silent, and Orientation Lock. Below these buttons, there is a brightness control; you drag the bar left or right to increase or decrease the brightness level on the screen. You can also place a check in the Auto box to allow the Galaxy Tab to adjust the brightness based on the light level it detects at your current location.

FIGURE 2.9   The Notifications tool offers more customization.

Tapping any of these buttons toggles the associated service on or off. For example, when you want to use the built-in GPS, you can turn it on here by tapping it once; the button turns green. Because GPS (and the Bluetooth and Wi-Fi services) consumes more battery power when it's turned on, this is a useful way to disable a service and save power when you don't need to have a service running.

Below the brightness adjustment bar, you find a listing of notifications from any apps that are capable of sending a message to the Notifications area. Figure 2.10 shows an alert that lets me know a few new (unread) email messages have arrived to my Gmail account. (These notifications can be cleared by tapping the Clear button, but after you clear them, they're gone for good.)

FIGURE 2.10   Emails, reminders, and other alerts will appear here.

TIP: **Open and Close Notifications from the Status Bar**

Along the top of the Galaxy Tab, the status bar displays the date, time, battery strength, and other notifications. Another method for opening Notifications is to hold your finger on the status bar and drag it to the bottom of the screen. To close it, just tap at the bottom of the Notification window and drag it up to the top of the screen.

Customizing Home Pages

Another suggestion for customizing your Galaxy Tab is to modify your home pages to display those apps that you use the most and remove apps that you don't find useful. You can also modify your home page's wallpaper to display a photo or other image stored on your device.

Figure 2.11 shows a basic home page with no app icons on it other than the Shortcut area at the bottom of the screen with icons for Browser, Gmail, and a button to view all my installed apps.

FIGURE 2.11   One home page screen with no apps and the default wallpaper.

Let's first change the background wallpaper. Tap the **Menu** button and select **Wallpaper**. Figure 2.12 shows the window that appears, enabling you to browse your Gallery (for photos), a set of animated wallpapers (called Live Wallpaper), or a handful of static wallpapers provided by your carrier.

I cover using your Gallery in Lesson 6, "Using the Gallery," but for now let's change the background to a Live Wallpaper. Tap **Live Wallpapers** to see a screen like the one in Figure 2.13.

ALERT: **Animation and the Battery**

Believe it or not, the small bit of animation in the Live Wallpapers does affect battery power. Because the screen is constantly having to refresh to create the animation, you experience a slight increase in battery drain.

FIGURE 2.12   Three options are available for wallpaper.

FIGURE 2.13   Live Wallpapers provide a small amount of animation.

If you choose to use the **Wallpaper Gallery** option, scroll through the provided high-resolution images to preview them at the top of the screen and tap the **Set Wallpaper** button to apply your selection.

Figure 2.14 shows a new wallpaper that I've applied. In this figure, I've also clicked the Menu button to pull up the six options to show you how easy it is to customize the home page that appears by default and the apps that appear on these home pages. Note that in Figure 2.14 I'm starting with a clean screen (the three shortcut icons at the bottom and obscured by the Menu pop-up window).

FIGURE 2.14　A new wallpaper and preparing to add some apps.

See the Edit button in Figure 2.14? Tap it and you see a screen like the one in Figure 2.15 that shows you all your customizable home pages and enables you to set one as the default Home screen that appears when you turn on your Galaxy Tab or click the **Home** button.

Tap the big plus (+) button to add a new home screen. You can have up to nine home screens. To navigate between home screens, drag your finger left or right on the screen to move from one to another, or touch the dots at the top of the screen to jump to one. A number is displayed at the top of the screen to indicate which home screen is selected. Figure 2.16 shows that I've added two home screens (for a total of six) and that I'm currently viewing home screen number five.

FIGURE 2.15   View all available screens and select a home screen.

Now let me show you how to customize a home screen. I've already selected home screen 5 (see Figure 2.16) so now I want to add some app shortcuts and a few other items. I have two ways to do this: I can press the **Menu** button and then select the **Add** option, or I can hold my finger down for 2 seconds on any empty area of the screen. Either method pulls up a window like the one in Figure 2.17.

You have four choices of things to add to a home screen: widgets, short-cuts, folders, and wallpapers. You're already familiar with the Wallpaper option (clicking the **Wallpapers** option takes you back to the screen in Figure 2.12), so let's look at widgets first. Tapping **Widgets** pulls up the screen shown in Figure 2.18.

FIGURE 2.16   You can have up to nine home screens.

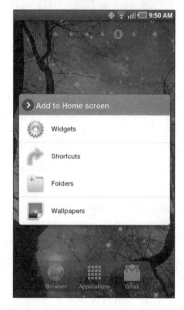

FIGURE 2.17   Add shortcuts, widgets, and more to a home screen.

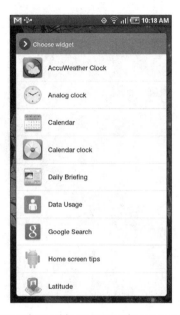

FIGURE 2.18   Adding various widgets to your home screens.

A widget is an interactive app that sits on the home screen. It can display information (such as stocks you want to follow or the current weather in your area) and it can also accept requests such as Google search terms or app searches in the Android Market (see Lesson 7, "Shop the Android Market"). To place a widget on the screen, just click a widget in the list and it appears on the current home screen. Figure 2.19 shows that I've selected the Google search toolbar. (Tap and hold a widget to drag it around the screen—remove your finger to drop it and lock it in place).

Figure 2.20 shows that I've added a shortcut to the Wi-Fi settings option and a folder that gains me access to all my contacts.

If you choose to add a shortcut, you see a screen like the one shown in Figure 2.21, giving you access to a variety of items that can be displayed on the screen and accessible with a single touch. (A faster way to add a shortcut is to tap and hold your finger on an app—a shortcut is automatically placed on the home screen.)

FIGURE 2.19   Drop a widget on the screen and drag it into place.

FIGURE 2.20   More items added to the home screen.

FIGURE 2.21   Select a shortcut to add to a home screen.

Finally, if you've added a widget, shortcut, or folder that you want to remove from a home screen, tap and hold the item until the Remove box appears in the lower part of the screen, as shown in Figure 2.22.

While continuing to hold down on the item, drag it to the Remove box and lift your finger. The item is removed from the home screen.

TIP: **Removing Is Not Deleting**

Removing a folder, shortcut, or widget from a home screen is not the same as deleting it completely. I show you how to permanently delete items such as apps in Lesson 7.

FIGURE 2.22   Remove an item by holding it down with your finger.

Summary

In this lesson, you learned how to customize your Galaxy Tab's screen by adding widgets, shortcuts, and other items. You also learned how to configure notifications such as email and reminder alerts. Finally, you learned how to use the Settings tool to configure dozens of settings such as display, sound, and Wi-Fi connectivity.

LESSON 3

Taking Photos and Video

In this lesson, you learn how to take photos and video with the Galaxy Tab and how to view, edit, save, and delete these files.

The Camera App

To take photos or videos with the Galaxy Tab, you use the Camera app that comes with your device. This app might be located on one of your home pages, or it might be located in the Applications section, or both. Figure 3.1 shows my Camera app on the first Applications page in the upper-right corner of the screen.

FIGURE 3.1   The Camera app enables you to take photos and video.

NOTE: **Camera Settings Can Be Tricky**

This chapter does not cover camera topics such as ISO settings, exposure, white balance, and other technical considerations that must be made when taking photos. If you need assistance with configuring the camera for taking the best photos, consult a beginner's guide on photography or visit http://en.wikipedia.org/wiki/Photography for more information.

It's simple to use: Just touch the app with your finger, and you see the Camera's user interface, as shown in Figure 3.2.

Shutter Button

FIGURE 3.2   The Camera app has a simple user interface.

The viewscreen is in the center of the screen, with camera options running down the left side of the screen (more on those shortly) and camera controls on the right side.

Taking a Photo

To take a photo, hold your Galaxy Tab up and use the viewscreen to find your subject. When you're ready to take the picture, simply tap the

Shutter button (see Figure 3.2), and the sound of a camera shutter confirms the photo has been taken.

A small thumbnail displays in the lower-right corner of the viewscreen showing a tiny image of your newest photo. Tap your finger on the photo to have access to five options: Share, Set As, Delete, Zoom, and View Next Photo. The following sections describe how these five options work. (If the options disappear, just tap on the displayed image again to make the options reappear.)

Delete

Tapping the **Delete** option presents you with a confirmation window, as shown in Figure 3.3. Tap the **OK** button to delete the photo, or tap the **Cancel** button to keep the photo.

FIGURE 3.3   Deleting a photo permanently removes it from the device.

Zoom

Use the **Zoom In** and **Zoom Out** buttons in the upper-right corner of the screen to enlarge and shrink the photo. Figure 3.4 shows the photo from Figure 3.3 enlarged. You can also use the pinch technique to enlarge and shrink an image. To enlarge, put your thumb and pointer finger together, touch the image, and then move the thumb and pointer finger apart.

FIGURE 3.4   Enlarge or shrink a photo using the Zoom In and Zoom Out options.

Likewise, to shrink an image, touch the image with the thumb and pointer finger (separated) and pinch them together.

Share

Selecting the **Share** option presents you with a new menu like the one shown in Figure 3.5. You can choose to share the photo using email,

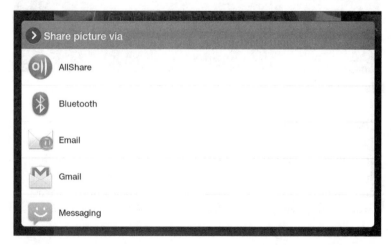

FIGURE 3.5   You can share your digital photos via email or other apps.

instant messaging, or any other service/app you have installed on your Galaxy Tab that supports sending digital files. If you have multiple apps that can send files, scroll down the page to view all your options.

For example, selecting **Email** opens your Email app, enabling you to send the photo along with a message and subject, as shown in Figure 3.6.

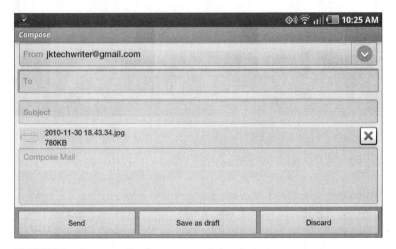

FIGURE 3.6   Use your Email app to send the photo to a contact.

Set As

Selecting the **Set As** option enables you to use the digital photo as either the wallpaper for your Galaxy Tab or as the icon for one of your contacts, as shown in Figure 3.7.

If you select the **Contact** option, you can then scroll down the list of your contacts and assign the photo as a contact icon. This option works best when you've taken a digital photo with your Galaxy Tab of the contact and can immediately assign it to that person's information in your Contacts app.

Choosing the **Wallpaper** option enables you to crop the image before placing it on the Galaxy Tab screen as the default wallpaper. Crop the image by holding your finger to the square's edge and dragging out or in to enlarge or shrink the box to the desired size. You can also move the box

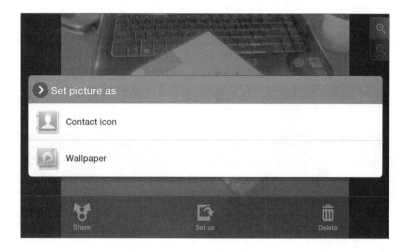

FIGURE 3.7   A photo can be used as a contact icon or as wallpaper.

by touching inside its border and dragging it to a desired location, as shown in Figure 3.8. Tap the **Save** button to keep your edits and use the image as the wallpaper or tap the **Discard** button to cancel the action.

FIGURE 3.8   Crop a photo to use as your Galaxy Tab's wallpaper.

View Next Photo

If you've taken numerous photos with the Camera app, you can use the **View Next Photo** buttons on either side of the photo (see Figure 3.9) to sort through them (and apply any options previously described).

FIGURE 3.9   Use the View Next Photo buttons to sort through your images.

To return to Camera mode, you must relaunch the Camera app from within the Applications group.

Camera Settings

Along the left side of the viewscreen, five icons represent different camera settings you can change, as shown in Figure 3.10. From top to bottom, they are Shooting Mode, Scene Mode, Flash, Exposure, and Settings.

For the Shooting mode, you can select to take a single shot, a set of continuous photos, a panoramic shot, a close-up smile shot, or a self-portrait. Tap the **Shooting Mode** icon shown in Figure 3.11 and select the option you want to use for Shooting mode.

Tap the **Scene Mode** icon (**SCN**), as shown in Figure 3.12, and you can choose from Portrait, Landscape, Night, and Sports options.

Camera Setting Options

FIGURE 3.10   Camera settings can be changed to modify your photos.

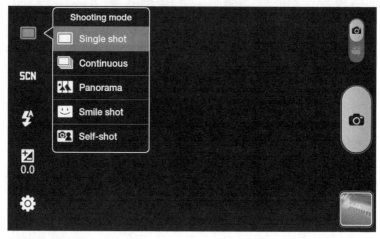

FIGURE 3.11   The Shooting mode offers a variety of photo types.

The flash settings shown in Figure 3.13 enable you to toggle the flash on or off or leave it set to Auto if you're uncertain about lighting requirements.

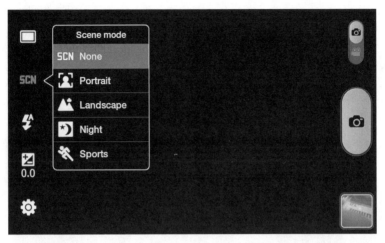

FIGURE 3.12 The Scene mode is useful for specifying the conditions under which photos are taken (inside, outside, nighttime, or fast-moving subjects).

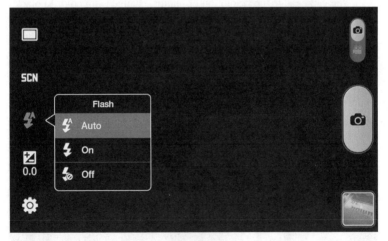

FIGURE 3.13 Flash options include On, Off, or Automatic.

You can tweak the exposure of the camera by sliding the control shown in Figure 3.14 up and down. You have to experiment with this setting to determine the best exposure for your environment and subject.

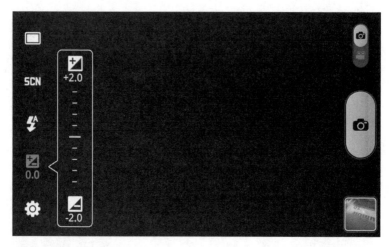

FIGURE 3.14 The Camera app enables you to modify the exposure setting.

Tapping the **Settings** icon pulls up a window like the one shown in Figure 3.15. You can change the resolution of photos, change from color to black and white (with the Effects option), change the ISO setting, and more from the Image tab. The Setup tab enables you to tweak items such as the shutter sound you hear when taking a photo, GPS coordinates embedded in the photos, and whether you want to review each photo after it is taken. After making your selections, tap the **Return** button on the Galaxy Tab to return to the Camera app's interface to take another photo.

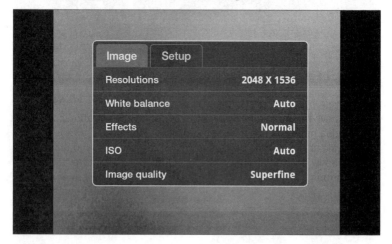

FIGURE 3.15 The Camera app offers even more settings to tweak.

Taking a Video

Taking a video is even simpler than taking a photo. You use the Camera app, but you first need to flip the Camera app to Video mode. To do this, tap the button indicated in Figure 3.16. This button toggles the Camera app between Photo and Video mode. After switching to Video mode, simply tap the **Record** button also indicated in Figure 3.16. Tap the **Record** button again to stop recording.

Switch between Photo and Video mode

Press to toggle between Record and Stop

FIGURE 3.16   Switch the Camera app to Video mode.

Video is stored in the Gallery app (see Lesson 6, "Using the Gallery," for more details) on your Galaxy Tab for later viewing. All the same editing features (Share, Delete, and so on) are available after you shoot a video by pressing the small thumbnail of the video in the lower-right corner of the Camera app's screen, and video settings can be tweaked using the icons along the left edge of the screen.

Summary

In this lesson, you were introduced to the Camera app and shown how to take photos. You also learned how to modify camera settings, edit individual photos, and take video.

LESSON 4

Web Browsing and Email

In this lesson, you learn how to use the Galaxy Tab browser to access the Web. You also learn to use the built-in Gmail app for use with your Google account and how to configure other types of email accounts.

Browsing the Web

To access Internet websites, you'll use the very handy Browser app that is conveniently located in the Primary Shortcuts area at the bottom of the screen (along with Applications and Gmail), as shown in Figure 4.1.

FIGURE 4.1 The Browser app is your path to the Web.

NOTE: **More Web Browsers**

If you're not happy with the Browser app that comes standard with the Galaxy Tab, you can find other web browsers with additional features in the Android Market. See Lesson 7, "Shop the Android Market," for more details on using the Android Market and for how to search for apps you want to install.

Touch the **Browser** app with your finger to launch. When it opens, you'll see an interface similar to the one shown in Figure 4.2, which shows the Browser app running with the Galaxy Tab rotated to maximize the web browser window.

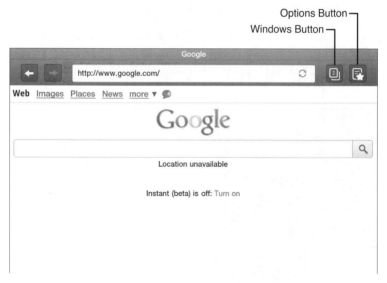

FIGURE 4.2 The Browser app displaying a page in Wide View.

If you rotate the Galaxy Tab to Normal View, the web browser rotates the onscreen image and provides scrollbars to navigate the page if portions of it extend beyond the screen's boundaries. Use the swipe gesture to scroll the page down and up and use the reverse-pinch gesture to enlarge an image or bit of text on the screen.

The Browser Interface

The Browser app's interface is quite simple: If you've used any web browser before, you'll find it easy to use. The special features are limited, but you might be surprised at how fast the pages load.

Visiting a Website

To enter a website, tap your finger inside the address bar, and a keyboard appears on screen, as shown in Figure 4.3.

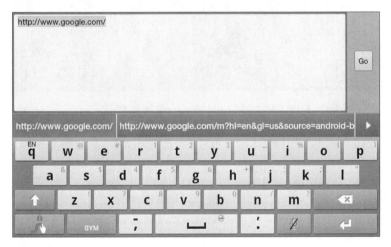

FIGURE 4.3 Type in a web address you want to visit.

The website loads and displays in the browser window. Tap the **Back** button to move to websites you previously visited, and tap the **Forward** button to move forward.

Moving Between Websites

If you enter a new web address on the current page you're viewing, the old page disappears and is replaced with the new one. If you want to save the website you're currently viewing and open a new web address so that you can flip back and forth, tap the **Windows** button (see Figure 4.2 for its location), and you see a screen like the one in Figure 4.4.

Tap the plus (+) sign in the upper-right corner to open a new web browser and enter the new address. Using this method, you can have multiple websites open, and you can simply tap on the website you want to visit to

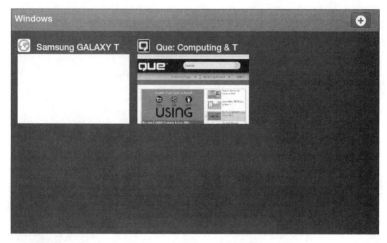

FIGURE 4.4　Jump from site to site with a single touch.

jump right to it. In Figure 4.4, I have two websites open: the Samsung website and the Que Publishing website.

Bookmarking a Site

If you find a website you visit frequently and want to save it (bookmark it), tap the **Options** button (see Figure 4.2), and a menu appears like the one shown in Figure 4.5.

FIGURE 4.5　Bookmark a site by tapping the **Options** button.

Tap the **Add Bookmark** button, and a new screen appears, as shown in Figure 4.6.

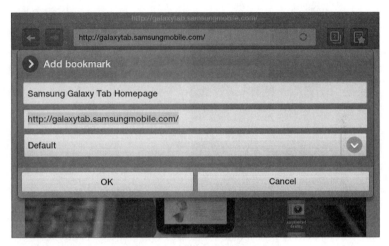

FIGURE 4.6   Provide details for your added bookmark.

As shown in Figure 4.6, you can provide a shorter name for the website to make it easer to find in your Favorites list. (The default is the full-length URL.) You can also tap the **Default** button to make it the website that always appears when you launch the Browser app.

Tap the **Edit** button (refer to Figure 4.5) and you can organize your bookmarks and delete any websites you want to remove.

Finally, if you tap the **Options** button again, you can tap the **Most Visited** tab to see the websites that have been viewed most frequently. Tap the **History** tab to view websites visited today, over the last week, or during the last month. Tap the **Clear** button to delete your browsing history.

Using Other Browser Options

While browsing a website, press the **Menu** button on the Galaxy Tab to see other options that are available (see Figure 4.7).

You can easily adjust the brightness, add a bookmark, and access the Browser Settings option by tapping the appropriate option. Click the **More** button if you want to send the web URL (link) to someone via email or instant messaging.

FIGURE 4.7   Additional options are available when using the Browser app.

The Download Manager option tracks any files you download from a website and offers a button (Go to My Files) that takes you to a folder where all your downloads are stored.

The Find on Page button enables you to search a web page for words or phrases that you are looking for. When the Browser app finds your search phrase, all instances of the word or phrase in the web page text appear in highlight.

Using Gmail

In Lesson 1, "The Setup Wizard," you learned how to set up your Galaxy Tab using the Setup Wizard. (If you haven't configured your Galaxy Tab to work with a Google user account, refer to Lesson 1 to do it now.) With your Google account, you can use Gmail to read and compose email messages.

To open and run the Gmail app, tap the **Gmail** icon (refer to Figure 4.1). It's best to use the Gmail app in Wide View mode (see Figure 4.8), but it also works in Narrow View mode.

Managing Email

The Gmail app offers access to many of Gmail's folders, including the Trash, Drafts, and All Mail folders. The Gmail app is a simple app, and its primary job is to provide access to your Inbox and enable you to compose, reply to, and forward emails, but you can access all Gmail's features if you know where to look and which buttons to tap.

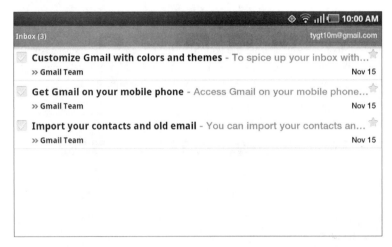

FIGURE 4.8   The Gmail app is customized just for Google email.

As you can see in Figure 4.8, your Inbox emails are listed vertically, most recent to oldest. Tap a message to open it. Figure 4.9 shows a message open for reading.

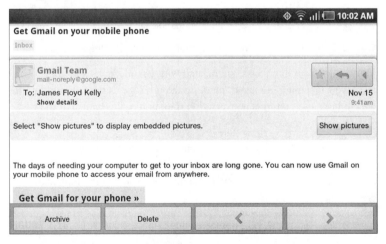

FIGURE 4.9   Tap an email message to read it.

From within an email, you have access to most of the Gmail app's features. You can tap the **Show Pictures** button to view any graphics that are part of the original message. Along the bottom of the screen are the buttons for filing the email (tap **Archive** to send it to Gmail's All Mail folder), deleting a message, and moving forward and backward within your Inbox.

To view additional tasks, tap the **Menu** button to show more options along the bottom of the screen, as shown in Figure 4.10.

FIGURE 4.10   Additional options are available while viewing a message.

You can perform many tasks associated with Gmail, such as modifying a message's label, adding a star, marking the message as unread, jumping to your Inbox, and muting a conversation (hiding it in the Inbox) of the Galaxy Tab.

Tap the **More** button if you want to report a message as spam, copy text from the message, and access the Gmail settings options that you can configure, such as adding an automated signature, changing the font size, and creating new labels.

NOTE: **Get Gmail Help**
If you're not familiar with Gmail's special features, such as labels or stars, tap the **Help** option (open a message, tap the Menu button, and then click the More option) to receive more details than I can offer in this short lesson.

Tap the **Go to Inbox** button to compose an email message and send it with an attachment, as described in more detail in the next section.

Composing a Message

While viewing your Inbox (refer to Figure 4.8), tap the **Menu** button and tap the **Compose** button. A new email message window opens like the one in Figure 4.11. Type the email address of your recipient into the To box, enter a subject, and then type a message.

FIGURE 4.11   Compose an email with a subject and a recipient.

When you've finished, tap the **Send** button. You may also tap the **Save as Draft** button to put the message in the Drafts folder, or you may tap the **Discard** button to delete the message and return to the Inbox.

How do you view the Drafts folder (or other Gmail folders) if you've saved a message? Just press the **Menu** button while viewing the contents of the Inbox and tap the **Go to Labels** button (refer to Figure 4.8). A page of folders displays, and you can scroll up and down the page to select a Gmail folder (such as Drafts or Trash or other) and view its contents.

The Gmail app is a useful app, with all the functionality and features available while using Gmail on a full-size computer or laptop. Because of the limited screen size provided by the Galaxy Tab, the Gmail app keeps many features hidden away, but all the features are there if you get used to using the Menu button and its many options.

Not everyone uses Gmail, though, which is why the Galaxy Tab also offers support for additional email providers, such as Yahoo!, Hotmail, AOL, and even Microsoft Exchange.

Using Other Email Services

If you want to configure other email services on the Galaxy Tab, you need to access the Setup Wizard again. From a home page, tap the **Menu** button and choose Settings. Scroll down the Settings screen and tap the **Setup Wizard**. You're likely to see a screen like the one in Figure 4.12 if you've

FIGURE 4.12　Access the Setup Wizard to add new email accounts.

configured a Google user account already. (You can also open up the Email app in the Applications group and use this app to add new email addresses and other email services such as Yahoo! and Hotmail.)

Tap the **Skip** button to see the choices of accounts you can synchronize with your Galaxy Tab (see Figure 4.13).

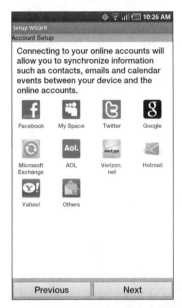

FIGURE 4.13   You can add other email services to your Galaxy Tab.

Select an icon on the screen, such as Yahoo! or Hotmail, to configure that particular email service. Figure 4.14 shows the screen that appears after clicking the Yahoo! icon.

Follow the steps and provide the information requested. Tap **Next** to move through the Setup Wizard for each email account you want to configure, and then tap **Done** to finish up the email account setup.

FIGURE 4.14   Setting up a Yahoo! email account on the Galaxy Tab.

NOTE: **Special Information Required**

You might be asked to provide information that you are not familiar with. If you are asked for a piece of information that you do not have, contact your email provider or tech support for that information. For example, if you want to add a Microsoft Exchange email account, you must provide information such as domain and the name of the Exchange server, two things you can get from your network administrator.

After providing a Yahoo! username and password (and clicking **Next**), you see a screen that enables you to provide a more descriptive name for the account (in this case, My Yahoo Email) and name that is displayed on outgoing messages (see Figure 4.15). Tap the **Done** button after you've entered the information.

FIGURE 4.15 Finish setting up an email account.

To view the new email account on your Galaxy Tab, tap the **Applications** button on a home page and find the Email app, as shown in Figure 4.16.

FIGURE 4.16 The Email app is used to access non-Gmail email.

Figure 4.17 shows the Inbox of my new Yahoo! account. The Email app is easy enough to figure out—tap a message to read it, use the **Menu** button to view available options, and tap the buttons along the top edge to move an email, delete it, forward it, or compose a new message.

FIGURE 4.17   Viewing your Inbox using the Email app.

Every email service (Hotmail, Exchange Server, Yahoo!, AOL) operates a little differently, so you have to play around with the Menu button and any other app buttons you find to understand their functionality.

Also, remember that the Notification Bar is useful for alerting you to incoming emails, especially when you are monitoring multiple email accounts. To access the Notification Bar, simply tap and hold your finger on the Status Bar along the top of the LCD screen, and drag your finger to the bottom of the screen and release.

Summary

In this lesson, you learned how to use the Browser app and many of its features, including the ability to add a bookmark and open new websites without closing others. You also learned how to use the Gmail and Email apps to view email and manage your messages.

LESSON 5

Exploring with GPS

In this lesson, you learn how to use your Galaxy Tab to navigate with the built-in GPS feature. You also learn how to find directions from one location to another.

Getting Started with Navigation

Your Galaxy Tab comes with a free app called Navigation. The best way to understand how Navigation works is simply to use it. Open the app from the Applications group. You might see a pop-up alert like the one in Figure 5.1. Tap the **OK** button to continue.

FIGURE 5.1   Navigation requires that the GPS feature be enabled.

In Figure 5.2, you're basically being asked to specify which service will assist your Galaxy Tab in determining your current location. You can choose the Google Location Services or your carrier (Verizon, in my case) and its location services. Another option is simply to use the Standalone GPS feature.

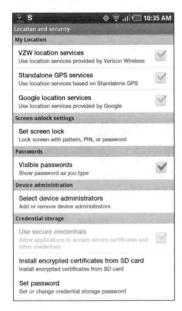

FIGURE 5.2   Select a location service for added features.

For purposes of this chapter, I use both Google Location Services and the Standalone GPS feature. (Be aware that using the Google Location Services or your carrier's version might provide additional features not covered in this lesson.)

After enabling both the Google Location Services and the Standalone GPS feature, close down Navigation and restart the app.

When you restart the app, it takes a moment for Navigation to determine your current location. After the app has determined your location, you can use the features of the app, such as the driving directions. Enter your desired destination by using the Speak Destination option when driving (see Figure 5.3) or use the Type Destination option (see Figure 5.4).

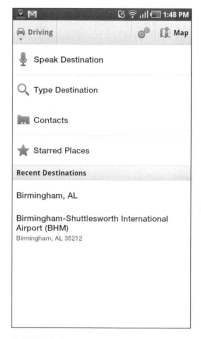

FIGURE 5.3 Use Navigation to get directions and map access.

FIGURE 5.4   Get driving directions by specifying a destination.

Navigation consults Google Maps (or your carrier's choice of map provider), and the screen changes to show your current location and a Map View with a solid green line indicating the direction you should go (see Figure 5.5).

Tapping the **Follow the Route** button at the top of the screen makes the screen change slightly (it shows your orientation relative to the direction you need to start moving), and a bit of text displays at the top of the screen to tell you which direction to drive.

Tapping the right-pointing arrow (to the right of the written instructions) enables you to view the next part of your journey. Notice in Figure 5.6 that the screen has changed to show where you'll be on the road and the next road you should look for.

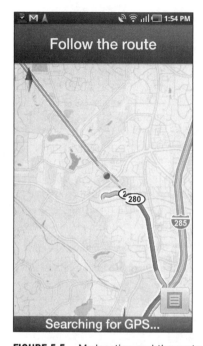

FIGURE 5.5 My location and the route I should take to my destination.

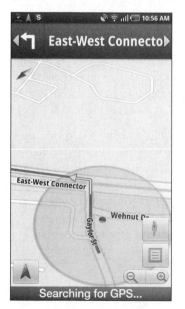

FIGURE 5.6 The next set of instructions for my journey.

NOTE: **When GPS Needs Help**

You might have noticed at the bottom of the screen that the text says "Searching for GPS." As I write this, it's a rainy day in Atlanta, Georgia. GPS functionality is questionable (in bad weather, signals from the GPS satellites aren't as reliable), so my Galaxy Tab is using the partnered Google Location Services to assist me. My Galaxy Tab was able to determine my location with the basic GPS service before losing signal. After the signal is re-obtained, my location on the LCD screen will update to show a more exact position.

For driving purposes, the Galaxy Tab's Navigation app can use Wi-Fi or 3G data connections to figure out my current position (using addresses of well-known locations) and update it on the map to still provide me with decent (but not always 100% accurate) driving instructions!

In addition to the map and driving instructions, Google Location Services offers some other features. The first is Road View. Tap the icon of a stick-man in the lower-right corner of the map to receive an image of your approximate location. This is great for helping identify landmarks, restaurants, and other buildings (see Figure 5.7).

Tap the blue arrow pointing up in the lower-left corner of the map to return to a bird's eye view of your location. Tap the **Follow the Route** button at the top to continue where you left off.

Another option available to you with Google Location Services is turning off the driving map and instead using text-based driving instructions. Tap the icon in the lower-right corner just beneath the Road View icon. You are provided with a list of driving instructions, as shown in Figure 5.8.

This list of text-based instructions is scrollable, enabling you to view all the turns and roads you'll encounter during your trip. At the top of the screen, the app estimates the number of miles you need to travel and the total travel time.

Tap the Galaxy Tab's **Return** button to go back to the Map View.

FIGURE 5.7   The Road View helps you identify landmarks and turns to make.

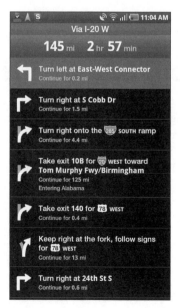

FIGURE 5.8   Text-based driving instructions can replace the Map View.

You can use the **Zoom In** and **Zoom Out** buttons at the bottom of the screen to enlarge or shrink the Map View. Doing so proves useful for seeing actual road names on the Map View, as shown in Figure 5.9.

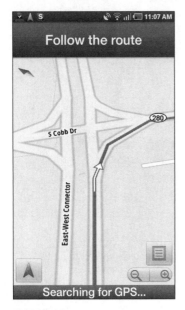

FIGURE 5.9   Zoom in to see road names and more detail.

Tap the **Menu** button to see a list of options like the ones in Figure 5.10.

The Search option enables you to search for keywords such as restaurant and hotel names and street addresses. Use the **Route Info** button to see a zoomed-out image of your complete journey, as shown in Figure 5.11. This is a useful view for seeing real-time traffic updates. (A green line indicates normal traffic flow at the posted speed limits, but yellow and red may indicate congestion or accidents.)

FIGURE 5.10   More options are built in to the Navigation app.

FIGURE 5.11   View your entire journey using the Route Info option.

The Layers option is an interesting feature. Tap it and a menu like the one in Figure 5.12 appears.

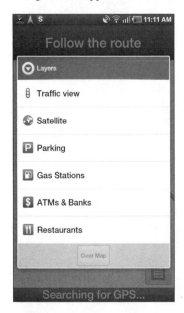

FIGURE 5.12   Layers can show gas stations, ATMs, and more along your path.

Tapping the **ATMs & Banks**, **Gas Stations**, or **Restaurants** options shows you these locations along your travel path, as shown in Figure 5.13. Note that gas stations are indicated by a small gas pump icon, restaurants by a small knife and fork icon, and ATMs are represented by $. You can toggle these options on or off by going back to the Layers button.

Although not very useful when it comes to driving, the Satellite option offers a fun and interesting view of your travel path. Figure 5.14 shows the Satellite option enabled.

FIGURE 5.13   Find useful resources as you travel.

FIGURE 5.14   Satellite View is pretty, but not useful when driving.

Tap the screen to zoom in and out on the Satellite View. When you've finished, remember to turn it off to return to Map View.

The Mute button disables the voice instructions that you hear if the volume on your Galaxy Tab is turned up.

Finally, you can exit the Navigation app by tapping the **Exit** button.

Having Fun with Places

If your Galaxy Tab offers the Places app, it's a nice app to use in conjunction with Navigation. (If you don't have the Places app, it's a free download from Android Market.) Places is a great little app that works in conjunction with GPS to provide you with the locations of services such as gas stations, ATMs, restaurants, and more. It's searchable, and you can even add your own categories (such as sporting goods stores or repair shops).

Figure 5.15 shows the Places app and the services it offers.

While Navigation is running, you see your current location at the bottom of the screen. At any time during your travels, you can tap any of the icons to view information about restaurants, hotels, ATMs, and more.

Figure 5.16, for example, shows a list of all the coffee shops in my area (including the one I'm sitting in as I write this lesson).

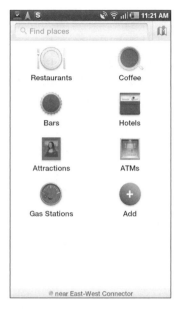

FIGURE 5.15 Use Places for more details about places to stop.

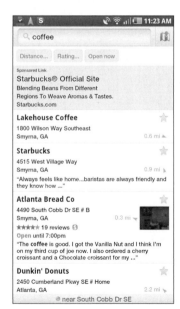

FIGURE 5.16 Plenty of places to get a coffee in my area.

Summary

In this lesson, you learned how to use the Navigation app to get directions from your current location to a specified destination, including traffic reports and satellite views along your path of travel. You also learned how to locate gas stations, ATMs, and more using the Places app.

Using the Gallery

In this lesson, you learn how to access, view, edit, and delete the photos and videos you have taken using the Camera app.

Accessing the Gallery

To view the photos and videos that you've taken with your Galaxy Tab, you need only access the Gallery app. You can find it in the Applications group, but many Galaxy Tabs are configured to have the Gallery app on one of the preconfigured home screens. Tap the **Gallery** app, and (if you've taken a few photos and a few videos) you should see a screen similar to the one in Figure 6.1.

FIGURE 6.1 The Gallery app home screen.

NOTE: **Screen Captures**

To take a snapshot of your Gallery Tab screen, just tap and hold your finger on the **Return** button before pressing the **Power/Lock** key. If the volume is turned up sufficiently, you should hear the familiar shutter sound and see a small black bar appear at the bottom of the screen informing you that the screenshot has been saved.

As you can see in Figure 6.1, the Gallery app saves photos and videos under the Camera group. Any screen captures you've taken are stored in the ScreenCapture group.

After the Gallery app is open, there are a few controls that might be of interest to you. First, in the upper-left corner of the screen is a small icon that looks like a small square photo (see Figure 6.2). Press this icon any

Return to Gallery home screen   Launch Camera app

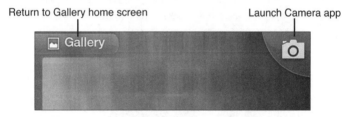

FIGURE 6.2   The shortcut to jump back to the Gallery app home screen.

time you're viewing photos or videos to go back to the Gallery app home screen in Figure 6.1.

Next, in the upper-right corner of the screen (refer to Figure 6.1) is a camera icon. Tapping this button immediately launches the Camera app (see Lesson 3, "Taking Photos and Video").

Tap your finger on the **Camera** group. (The number in parentheses tells you how many photos and videos are stored in the group.) Figure 6.3 shows the screen that opens, displaying your photos in one of two different configurations. You can also tap the **ScreenCapture** group to view your screen captures. (The controls described in this section work the same no matter which group you are viewing.)

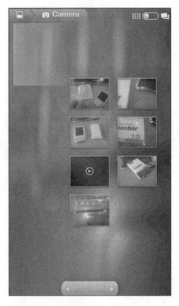

FIGURE 6.3 The Camera group shows videos and photos you've taken.

The first possible configuration is shown in Figure 6.3 and displays thumb-nails of your photos and videos in a series of rows and columns. You drag your finger left or right to move back and forth to view the thumbnails.

To switch to the other configuration, tap the **Toggle** button in the upper-right corner of the screen (refer to Figure 6.3). Now, instead of rows and columns, the thumbnails are grouped in stacks that are divided by date and time, as shown in Figure 6.4.

To help you identify which group of photos you're viewing, the name of the group appears to the right of the shortcut icon in the upper-left corner of the screen (refer to Figure 6.4). Remember that you can tap the shortcut icon (the small photo icon) to go back to the Gallery home screen.

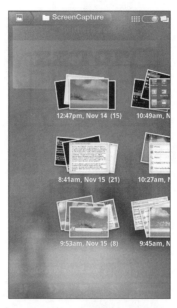

FIGURE 6.4 Stacks of images are grouped by date and time.

FIGURE 6.5 Photos and videos can be viewed in Vertical mode.

> NOTE: **Configuration Toggle 2**
> You can always toggle back and forth between views using the
> **Toggle** button in the upper-right corner, but tapping the name of the
> group you're viewing does the same thing.

Finally, instead of swiping your finger left or right on the screen to sift
through your photos and videos, you can use the drag bar at the very bottom of the screen (refer to Figure 6.3). Simply hold your finger to the drag
bar and drag left or right to move the collection on the screen. (This won't
be useful if you have fewer than 10 thumbnails on the screen.)

Viewing a Photo or Video

When you're viewing a group of photos or videos, simply tap a thumbnail
to view that image in a full-screen view. Figure 6.5 shows a photo opened
while the Tab is in Vertical mode. Notice that the photo does not display
using the full size of the LCD screen.

Rotate the Galaxy Tab to Widescreen mode, and the photo expands to fill
more of the screen, as shown in Figure 6.6.

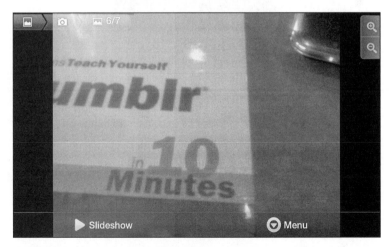

FIGURE 6.6   Rotate the Galaxy Tab to view photos in Widescreen mode.

Manipulating Your Photos and Videos

In either Vertical or Widescreen mode, you have access to some new tools. Tap the photo to toggle the available tools on and off. Figure 6.5 shows the screen without the tools, and Figure 6.7 shows the same photo with the tools enabled.

FIGURE 6.7   Tools appear onscreen above and below the image.

The first tool, visible in the upper-left corner of the screen just after the shortcut and group icon, is the photo/video counter. In Figure 6.7, I can tell that I'm viewing the sixth of seven photos in the selected group (6/7). What's the group name? Tap the counter and it toggles back and forth between the counter and the name of the group you're currently viewing.

In the upper-right corner of the screen, you also see icons for zooming in and out of the image. You can also double-tap an image to zoom in and out quickly as well as use the pinch technique described earlier in Lesson 3.

Along the bottom of the screen are the Slideshow and Menu buttons. Tapping the **Slideshow** button provides a quick display of all photos or videos in the current group you're viewing.

Tap the **Menu** button once and you see a screen like the one in Figure 6.8.

FIGURE 6.8   You can share and delete photos with a single click.

Tap the **Share** button to see a list of apps (such as Gmail or Messaging) for sharing the current image with others or via a file-sharing service such as Picasa.

Tap the **Delete** button to delete the current image. Tap the **Confirm Deletions** button to delete the photo or video, or tap the **Cancel** button if you don't want to delete it.

Editing Photos

Tap the **Menu** button once more to see a pop-up menu like the one in Figure 6.9.

FIGURE 6.9   Perform basic edits on your photos.

Tapping the **Details** button enables you to view information such as the date and time the photo was taken and GPS details if that feature is enabled (see Lesson 5, "Exploring with GPS"). Tap the **OK** button when you have finished.

Tapping the **Set As** button enables you to use the current image as wallpaper or as a contact icon.

The Crop button enables you to drag a box to a portion of the photo that you want to save as a separate photo. You can increase the height and width of the box by dragging its edges left or right or up and down to increase the size (see Figure 6.10).

> TIP: **Crop a Photo**
> It's easier to crop a photo when the Galaxy Tab is in Widescreen mode. This mode provides you with a larger image on the screen and more space to expand the crop box.

FIGURE 6.10   Use the crop box to select a portion of the image.

Tap the **Save** button to save the photo with the changes you made or tap the **Discard** button.

Tap the **Print** button (see Figure 6.9) to choose a Wi-Fi–enabled printer to print your current photo selection.

NOTE: **Wi-Fi Printers**
When you tap the **Print** button, you are asked to locate a Wi-Fi printer using the Wi-Fi Settings screen. If no Wi-Fi printer is available, you cannot print the photo.

Finally, you can use the **Rotate Right** and **Rotate Left** buttons to rotate the current photo left or right 90 degrees.

Working with Video

Working with videos is slightly different from working with photos, and the options available to you are slightly more limited.

When you tap the thumbnail for a video, the video immediately launches and begins playing onscreen. Tap the **Menu** button to see a handful of options like the ones in Figure 6.11.

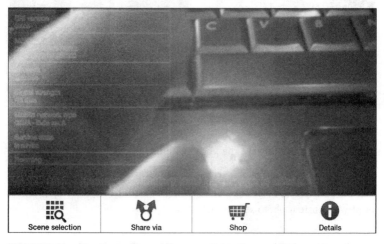

FIGURE 6.11   You have a few options available for your videos.

First, for longer videos, you can tap the **Scene Selection** button and view thumbnails of your video at various points in time. Figure 6.12 shows my short video is broken into 1-second intervals (not very useful, but for longer videos it can save you time when trying to jump to one particular scene). Tap a thumbnail and the video begins playing at that selected point in time.

You can also share your video by tapping the **Share Via** button. Figure 6.13 shows the four options available, including posting your video to YouTube (requires a YouTube account) and via instant messenger, Bluetooth (send a video to a friend's phone, for example), or the Samsung AllShare service that enables video to be played on Samsung Blu-Ray players wirelessly.

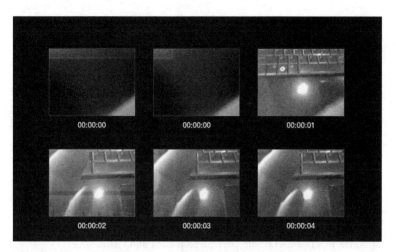

FIGURE 6.12   Jump to specific scenes by selecting a time.

FIGURE 6.13   Share your videos with others.

The Details button provides information such as the size, resolution, dura-
tion, and format of the video.

NOTE: **The Shop Option**

Figure 6.11 shows one other option: the Shop button. Tap the button, and nothing happens. What is this option? There doesn't appear to be any documentation on this feature, but it might be that Samsung intends to enable you at a later time to take a photo of a product's barcode and click the Shop button to have the product identified so that you can compare prices online and locally before purchasing.

Summary

In this lesson, you were shown how to view your photos and videos using the Gallery app. You were also shown how to perform some basic edits and how to share and delete your saved photos and video.

LESSON 7

Shop the Android Market

In this lesson, you learn how to search the Android Market for new apps, how to purchase an app (if a fee is required), and how to install an app. You also learn how to manage and delete apps.

The Android Market

You're not limited to just the handful of apps that came preinstalled on your Galaxy Tab. Thousands of apps are available for your Galaxy Tab, many of them free or at a low cost to purchase. To get these apps, though, you need to learn how to access and use the Android Market.

Fortunately, accessing the Android Market is simple: Just open the Applications group and click the **Market app** icon, shown in Figure 7.1.

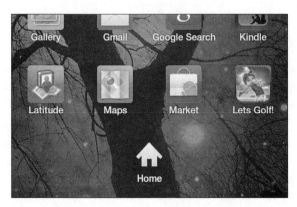

FIGURE 7.1   The Market app gets you to the Android Market.

When the Android Market opens, you see a screen similar to the one in
Figure 7.2. Your screen might look slightly different depending on the
company you purchased your Galaxy Tab from, but for the most part, the
app's search, purchase, and download features should work the same.

FIGURE 7.2   The Android Market has an easy-to-use interface.

In Figure 7.2, notice the screen is divided into sections. There's a menu
bar along the top that offers up an Apps button, a Games button, and possi-
bly a button for carrier-specific apps (in this case, Verizon Wireless apps).

At the bottom of the screen is a scrollable window (up and down) that lists
featured apps—these are popular apps that many users are downloading or
new apps of interest. This list changes often, so something you see listed
today might not be there tomorrow. For that reason, it's best to get used to
using the Apps button to view a list of the categories that apps fall under.

If you want to immediately search for an app using keywords, tap the text box in the top-right corner of the screen and enter some keywords to search the entire applications database for apps that fit your search criteria.

Tap the **Apps** button and you see a screen similar to the one in Figure 7.3.

FIGURE 7.3   You can search for apps using a variety of categories.

Category examples include Communication, Productivity, Sports, and Shopping. At the top of the list is the All Applications selection. Although this is useful, you might be overwhelmed by the list of available apps. For this reason, it's best to always tap a category before you begin searching for apps.

Our example is a search for a webcam app, which you can find under the Communication category (see Figure 7.4).

The name of the category displays at the top of the screen along with three buttons: Top Paid, Top Free, and Just In. When you're searching for something particular, though, you can use the Search feature in the top-right corner of the screen. In this case, however, the search is limited to the category you selected.

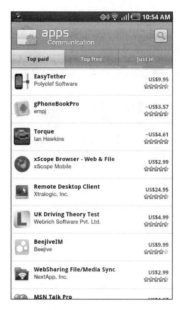

FIGURE 7.4   Searching a category for an app of interest.

Tapping the **Top Paid** button enables you to view a scrollable list of the most popular apps that have been purchased. Likewise, clicking the **Top Free** button provides a scrollable list of the most popular free apps. In both cases, you can see a rating of one to five stars to the right of each app's name. (The price of an app is located above the rating.)

Tapping the **Just In** button provides a scrollable list of new apps, many of them free and others for a price.

TIP: **Beware New Ratings**

New apps often have few ratings. Because ratings are an average of all reviews, always look over the reviews that have been submitted. An app with a one-star review and a five-star review displays a three-star average review, making it difficult to determine whether an app is really useful. That's when you have to read the current reviews and take a risk.

Examining an App

Using the scrollable list of apps, tap the name of an app to view more details about that app and to read comments. Figure 7.5 shows the details provided for the Skype application.

FIGURE 7.5   View details and comments for an app.

The About button displays a scrollable review of the app, including any special information about its functionality. You can also see how many users have downloaded the app and view its version number and size (in megabytes).

Tap the **Comments** button to see a scrollable list of reviews written by those who have downloaded and tested the app. Figure 7.6 shows why the Skype app has an average review of three stars; reviews range from "Poor call quality" to "Love the app" and everything in between.

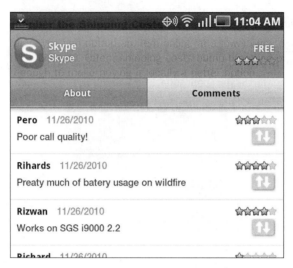

FIGURE 7.6   Reviews of apps can provide more details.

Downloading a Free App

If you decide to download a free app, tap the **Install** button (refer to
Figure 7.5). Some apps immediately begin downloading, but others might
provide an alert like the one in Figure 7.7.

As you can see in Figure 7.7, the Skype app accesses a mix of information
stored on my Galaxy Tab, including my contact database, the memory
card, my network connection, and more.

If you're okay with an app's alerts, tap the **OK** button to continue the
install. Otherwise, tap the **Cancel** button to return to the previous screen.
Figure 7.8 shows that the application is now being downloaded and
installed.

When the download and install is complete, you can check the
Notifications screen (see Lesson 2, "Configuration and Notifications") to
see a list of alerts as shown in Figure 7.9. (I downloaded the Star Traders
RPG game, as well.)

To access the newly downloaded app, open up the Applications group and
browse the apps. Figure 7.10 shows my two new apps, Skype and Star
Traders, ready to use.

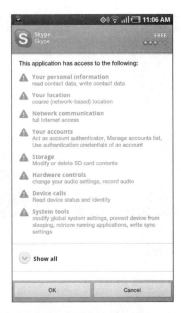

FIGURE 7.7   Read all app alerts before continuing with a download.

FIGURE 7.8   The download and installation begins.

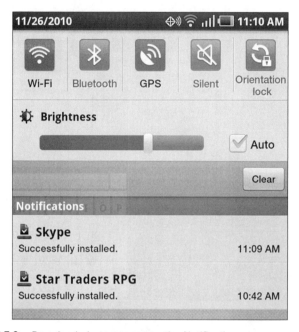

FIGURE 7.9 Download alerts appear on the Notification screen.

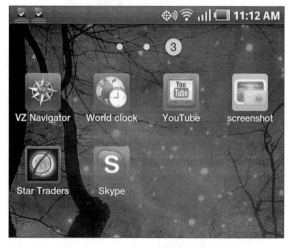

FIGURE 7.10 New apps appear in the Applications group.

TIP: **Status Bar Download Alerts**
Instead of checking the Notification screen, you can also see a small icon in the upper-left corner of the screen in Figure 7.10. Those small check marks indicate a download succeeded.

Purchasing an App

Although a lot of free apps are available for download, sooner or later you're going to find an app that you want that costs money. Fortunately, the price of most apps doesn't match up to the price of software you'd buy in a store. (Most apps can be purchased for less than $5, and the majority of apps costs only 99 cents.)

Figure 7.11 shows a game that I've found, Heavy Gunner 3D, and it's on sale for only 99 cents! (It was $4.99 and might have returned to that price by the time you read this.)

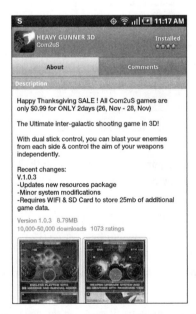

FIGURE 7.11   Locate an app you want to purchase and view its details.

Before you purchase an app, you can find out a bit more about it. If you scroll past the comments, you can view additional details, including screen captures and the developer's website and an email address if you have more specific questions. There might even be a phone number (but this isn't always the case). (See Figure 7.12.)

FIGURE 7.12   Contact and web information for an app.

If you decide to make a purchase after reviewing the website for more information, tap the **Buy** button. You should see a warning screen similar to the one in Figure 7.7. Tap the **OK** button to continue. Figure 7.13 shows the type of screen that appears next.

If you have a credit card on file with your Google user account, the last four digits appear (refer to Figure 7.13). Place a check in the box to indicate you agree with the terms of service for making a purchase from the Android Market.

If you want to use a different credit card, tap the down-pointing arrow to the right of your saved credit card and choose to use a different credit card.

FIGURE 7.13 The purchase summary screen.

When you're ready to purchase, tap the **Buy Now** button at the bottom of the screen. The screen now shows the purchase being authorized and a button at the bottom of the screen that you can use to cancel the download. Figure 7.14 shows the authorization screen.

When the purchase is complete, the download begins. You can view the status of a download on the Notification screen, as shown in Figure 7.15.

Uninstalling Apps

Downloading and installing apps is simple... and it can be addictive. There are so many free apps out there to try, and with the inexpensive nature of Android apps, you can quickly find your Applications group filling up fast with dozens and dozens of apps.

In addition to downloading and installing an app, you need to know how to uninstall apps that you no longer want to have stored on your Galaxy Tab. Here's how to perform this action.

FIGURE 7.14   The purchase must be approved before the download begins.

TIP: **Uninstall Versus Delete**

For most apps, you don't delete them; you simply uninstall them. When you purchase an app, you own it forever. This enables you to remove an app from your Galaxy Tab and then later reinstall it if you want to have it back.

First, tap the **Menu** button on your Galaxy Tab and choose the **Settings** option (refer to Lesson 2). Scroll down the list of Settings and tap the **Applications** category. Figure 7.16 shows the screen that opens.

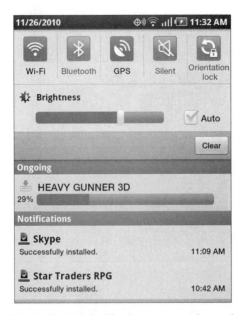

FIGURE 7.15 The application download process can be tracked.

FIGURE 7.16 The Applications Settings screen.

Next, tap the **Manage Applications** option. You see a screen similar to the one in Figure 7.17.

FIGURE 7.17   View only third-party apps on the Manage Applications screen.

Along the top of the screen are four buttons: Third Party, Running, All, and On SD Card.

The Third Party button shows all the apps that are not provided with the basic Android operating system. Notice in Figure 7.17 that the Let's Golf and Nova games were provided by my carrier (Verizon Wireless) and might not come with your Galaxy Tab. You can also see the four apps that I've downloaded (free or purchased): HeavyGunner, Screenshot, Skype, and Star Traders.

Tap the **All** button to see every app installed on your Galaxy Tab. Figure 7.18 shows the All button selected and the scrollable list of apps.

To uninstall an app, select it from the scrollable list. Figure 7.19 shows the application info for a selected app, which includes an Uninstall button at the top of the screen.

FIGURE 7.18 View all apps on the Manage Applications screen.

FIGURE 7.19 Uninstall an app by selecting it in the Manage Applications listing.

Tap the **Uninstall** button. You are given an opportunity to cancel the operation. If you want to continue, tap the **OK** button. The uninstall doesn't take long, and when it's finished you see a screen that tells you the uninstall was successful, like the one in Figure 7.20.

FIGURE 7.20   A successfully uninstalled app.

You are returned to the Manage Applications screen and can select more apps to be uninstalled. When you have finished uninstalling apps, tap the **Home** button to check the Applications group and verify that the uninstalled apps have had their icons removed.

Summary

In this lesson you learned how to use the Android Market. You also learned how to search for desired apps, purchase and download free and non-free apps, and install and uninstall apps.

LESSON 8

Making Phone Calls

In this lesson, you learn how to use the free Skype app to make phone calls (and instant message) from the Galaxy Tab to any other device running the same app.

Getting Started with Skype

One of the most popular apps around these days for device-to-device (laptop, desktop, Galaxy Tab, mobile phone, and so on) communication is Skype. It uses an Internet connection (Wi-Fi or other) to enable two parties to talk, free of charge (including country-to-country calls).

> TIP: **Video Calls**
> The Skype app also supports video chat—using a WebCam to place video calls between users. The Galaxy Tab version of Skype, however, does not currently support the video option. This might change, so be on the lookout for upgrades to the Skype app that enable video chat using your Galaxy Tab.

Most Skype users are familiar with it for PC-to-PC calls, but Skype has expanded its service to other devices, including the Galaxy Tab. This is a great feature because it means you can be speaking from your PC, laptop, Galaxy Tab, or mobile phone and the other Skype user can do the same.

Using Skype requires a user account; visit www.skype.com to learn more and to set up your Skype account, or just download the free Skype app from the Android Market and use the onscreen instructions in the app to create your Skype account.

Figure 8.1 shows the Skype app opening on the Galaxy Tab. When it first opens, it logs you in using your Skype username and saved password.

FIGURE 8.1   The Skype app logs you in automatically.

After the Skype app has logged you in, you are presented with the basic interface shown in Figure 8.2.

The Contacts tab (refer to Figure 8.2) is where all of your fellow Skype users are listed. The Call tab enables you to make phone calls to landlines (with a very small charge applied) and mobile phones. The My Info tab provides details on your account, including whether you are showing yourself as online (more on this in a moment) and any funds you've allocated to Skype Credit for making calls to non-Skype users' landlines and mobile phones.

The Events tab is where you find requests from other Skype users asking to be approved. If you approve a Skype user, you can make Skype calls to that person as well as receive Skype calls from that person. Figure 8.3 shows that a Contact Request has been received (from my home account). You can also see that I made a 2-minute call yesterday to another Skype user.

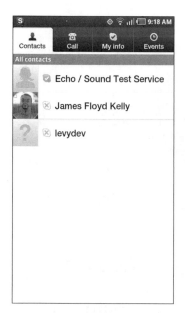

FIGURE 8.2 The Skype user interface includes four tabs.

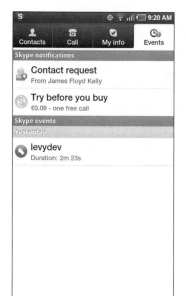

FIGURE 8.3 Approve users by clicking the Contact Request.

TIP: **Finding Skype Users**

To find other Skype users, press the **Menu** button, and then tap the **Add** button in the list of options. Type the name of the person you're looking for (or, if you know the Skype username, enter that) and tap the **Find** button. Scan the list of possible user accounts, and tap the one you want to call. When that user's information screen is displayed, tap the **Add** button in the lower-right corner of the screen and that person finds an alert the next time he opens Skype that asks him to approve (or deny) your request.

After you approve a user, that user's Skype account is listed on the Contacts tab, as shown in Figure 8.4.

Configure Your Skype Account

Your Galaxy Tab has a built-in camera, so it's now time to update your account with a picture and a status update, sort of a "What I'm doing right now" statement.

Tap the **My Info** tab, and then tap the **No Profile Picture Set** box. A pop-up window appears like the one in Figure 8.5.

You have three options for assigning a picture to your Skype account. The From Album option opens the Gallery (see Lesson 6, "Using the Gallery") and enables you to select an image. Use the crop function, and tap the **Save** button to assign the image to your Skype account.

The Take Picture option launches the Camera app and enables you to take a self-portrait (or other photo). Tap the **Clear** option to clear the photo and start over.

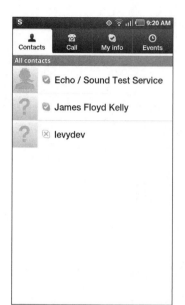

FIGURE 8.4 Approved Skype users appear on the Contacts tab.

FIGURE 8.5 Add a picture to your Skype account.

Figure 8.6 shows the selected image I've associated with my Skype account.

FIGURE 8.6   A picture assigned to my Skype account.

All that's left is to provide a "mood message" as Skype calls it. Tap in the text box just below your account name and type a short message, like the one shown in Figure 8.7.

Skype users who look at your account from their own Skype app see that message. Likewise, status messages of other users appear below their names on the Contacts tab, as shown in Figure 8.8.

FIGURE 8.7 Provide a status message for your Skype account.

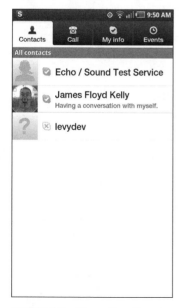

FIGURE 8.8 View other Skype user status messages.

Making a Call

After a Skype user is listed on the Contacts tab, it's a simple matter to call that person. But before you place a call, always check the status of a Skype user. Skype users can toggle their status to a variety of settings, including Online, Away, and Do Not Disturb; there's even an Invisible option. It's common courtesy to respect other users' status settings and not call them if they are listed as Away or Do Not Disturb.

Click the **My Info** tab shown in Figure 8.9 to view how your status is seen by other Skype users. (In Figure 8.9, you can see that the Status is listed as Online.)

FIGURE 8.9   View your Skype status on the My Info tab.

Tap the status (in this case, Online) and a pop-up window appears similar to the one in Figure 8.10, allowing you to change your status and how other Skype users see your account.

Assuming a contact's status is Online, it's time to make a phone call. Return to the Contacts tab and tap the name of a contact. That user's account page opens, as shown in Figure 8.11.

FIGURE 8.10   Set your status as Online, Away, or other.

FIGURE 8.11   Place a call or chat from a Skype user's account page.

Tap the **Call** button to make a call. Figure 8.12 shows the call being made.

FIGURE 8.12   A call being placed and waiting for an answer.

When the person you're calling answers, the call begins. You can talk, mute the microphone (with the icon in the lower-right corner), or mute the speaker on your Galaxy Tab (with the icon in the lower-left corner of the screen).

When someone calls you from his Skype account, an Incoming Call alert appears on your Galaxy Tab screen, as shown in Figure 8.13. You have two choices: Answer or Decline. Tap the appropriate button based on what you want to do.

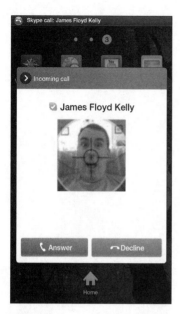

FIGURE 8.13   An incoming call: answer or decline?

Instant Messaging

In addition to making calls, you might also find Skype's Instant Messaging feature useful. It's nice for a quick chat when you don't feel like placing a phone call. Refer to Figure 8.11; instead of tapping the Call button for a Skype user, tap the **Chat** button. Figure 8.14 shows the screen that appears on the Galaxy Tab.

Use the onscreen keyboard to type your messages, as shown in Figure 8.15. Tap the **Return** button (to the right of the text field where you typed your message), and your message is added to the conversation.

Tap the **Menu** button to see two options: Add Participants and Call. Tapping the **Call** button ends the chat and immediately calls the person with whom you're chatting. Tapping the **Add Participants** button enables you to choose additional Skype users from the Contacts list and bring them into the chat discussion.

FIGURE 8.14   The Chat screen enables you to type your messages.

FIGURE 8.15   Type your messages using the onscreen keyboard.

To return to your Contacts list, tap the icon in the upper-left corner that looks like a small human head.

Summary

In this lesson, you learned how to use the free Skype app to make phone calls to other Skype users and how to use the Instant Messaging feature. You also learned how to update your Skype account with an image and status message.

Read Books, Listen to Music, and Watch Videos

In this lesson, you learn how to use three important apps with your Galaxy Tab: the Kindle eReader, the built-in Music Player, and the YouTube viewer.

Reading a Book

The Galaxy Tab comes preloaded with the Kindle app that enables you to purchase, download, and read digital versions of books and magazines. First let's take a look at some of the basics of using the Kindle app, including buying a book and downloading it to your device.

> **TIP: One Digital Book, Multiple Places to Read**
>
> When you purchase books from Amazon.com for use with the Kindle app, you can also read the book on your computer or an actual Kindle device (if you own one). For more details, visit www. amazon.com, and then click the Kindle menu on the left side of the screen. On the fly-out menu, you see a listing for Free Kindle Reading Apps that enables you to download readers for PC, Mac, BlackBerry, and other devices.

The first time you open the Kindle app, you are asked to tap the **Menu** button to buy a digital book (or magazine) from Amazon.com or download

existing digital books that you've already purchased. If you've never purchased a digital book from Amazon.com, you need to visit the Kindle
Store. Figure 9.1 shows the buttons available after tapping the Menu button. To purchase a book, tap the **Kindle Store** button.

FIGURE 9.1   The Kindle app enables you to read your digital books and
magazines.

Use the Kindle app's Search function to find a book you want to read. I've
typed in the keywords "Teach Yourself 10 Minutes" to find all the Pearson
books that have those words in the title, as shown in Figure 9.2.

Scroll down the list of results to find the book you want. After tapping the
book's cover, you see a page with more details on the book, including a
button for purchasing.

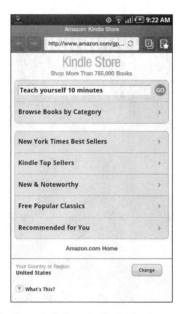

FIGURE 9.2   Use the Search feature to find a book.

If you have an Amazon.com account that enables you to use the 1-Click
option (a single click buys the book because your credit card and shipping
info is all saved under your account), you can make a purchase immediately. If you don't have a 1-Click account with Amazon.com, you are required
to create one (and log in) before using the 1-Click feature. After creating
the account, you might have to relaunch the Kindle app and search again
for a book if you're not automatically sent back to the purchase page. A
drop-down box below the Buy Now with 1-Click button enables you to
select the device you want to use for downloading. If you own other
devices where you've installed the Kindle app, these other devices also
appear in the drop-down menu. If you want to install on the Galaxy Tab,
leave the default setting as the SCH-1800 (for the Galaxy Tab).

Tap the **Buy Now with 1-Click** button, and a message notifies you that
your purchase is being downloaded. Tap the **Go to Kindle for Android**
button to return to the Kindle app home page, or tap the **Home** button and
reopen the Kindle app. Either way, the new purchase appears on the
Kindle app home screen, as shown in Figure 9.3.

FIGURE 9.3   Purchase a book and the download appears on the Kindle app home screen.

Tap the cover or title of the book to open the item. The first time you open a book, the app explains how you turn a page—a tap in a margin or a flick of a finger. Tapping in the center of the screen toggles the page scrollbar on and off (at the bottom of the page), and tapping the **Menu** button provides options such as placing a bookmark, changing the font, font size, or background color, and jumping to a specific location in the book (such as the table of contents).

Reading with the Kindle app is easy on the Galaxy Tab. It's like holding a paperback book, and a single swipe of your finger turns a page. The table of contents is fully hyperlinked; click a topic, as shown in Figure 9.4, and you jump straight to that page.

The Kindle app is a popular eReader, but it's not your only option. Visit the Android Market to find the Nook for Android app that enables you to view digital books you've purchased from Barnes & Noble. You can also search for Borders eBooks, an app that enables you to purchase and read digital content from the Borders bookstore.

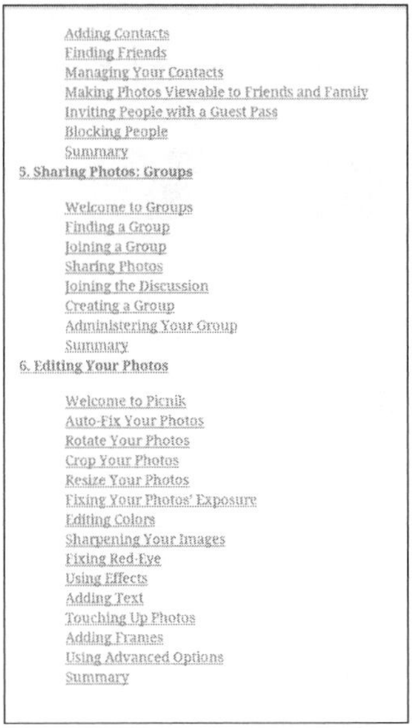

Adding Contacts
Finding Friends
Managing Your Contacts
Making Photos Viewable to Friends and Family
Inviting People with a Guest Pass
Blocking People
Summary
5. Sharing Photos: Groups

Welcome to Groups
Finding a Group
Joining a Group
Sharing Photos
Joining the Discussion
Creating a Group
Administering Your Group
Summary
6. Editing Your Photos

Welcome to Picnik
Auto-Fix Your Photos
Rotate Your Photos
Crop Your Photos
Resize Your Photos
Fixing Your Photos' Exposure
Editing Colors
Sharpening Your Images
Fixing Red-Eye
Using Effects
Adding Text
Touching Up Photos
Adding Frames
Using Advanced Options
Summary

FIGURE 9.4 View the table of contents and click a topic to jump to it.

There are many more eReaders out there to try. Because many books are often available from only one seller, you might find yourself installing a handful of eReader apps on your Galaxy Tab. Don't let this bother you; although features may differ slightly from eReader to eReader, the basic function of reading your digital books and magazines is the same.

Listening to Music

Your Galaxy Tab is a great device for reading books, but it's also a great way to listen to your music. You can find the Music Player app in the Applications group, and the first time you open it you're likely to find it empty. You need to load your Galaxy Tab up with your MP3 music files or purchase some online.

Figure 9.5 shows the Music Player open and ready for downloading some music.

The first thing you need to do is transfer some music to your Galaxy Tab. To do this, connect your Galaxy Tab to your computer (that's storing the MP3s) and mount the Galaxy Tab.

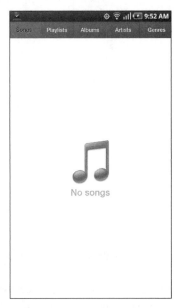

FIGURE 9.5   The Music Player is the app for listening to tunes.

TIP: **Connecting the Tab to a PC**

Connecting your Galaxy Tab to a computer requires mounting the device. For instructions on how to do this, see Lesson 10, "Helpful Tips and Useful App Suggestions." Steps for browsing the file structure of your Galaxy Tab are provided.

After mounting the Galaxy Tab, you're going to want to copy any MP3 music you want to have on your device to the Download folder, as shown in Figure 9.6.

FIGURE 9.6 Copy MP3 files to the Download folder on the Galaxy Tab.

Next, open the Music Player app to see your music organized on the Songs tab, as shown in Figure 9.7. (Music is listed alphabetically, but you can tap the **Artists** tab to view music organized by artist or the **Albums** tab to view by album title.)

Tap a song to hear it. You control the music with the volume drag bar at the top of the screen and the other music controls, such as pause and fast forward, at the bottom of the screen (see Figure 9.8).

If you tap the **Menu** button and tap the **Shop** option, you might be taken to your carrier's music service. My Galaxy Tab is from Verizon Wireless, which has an agreement with Rhapsody for purchasing music (see Figure 9.9). Your carrier might offer a different service; check with your carrier to find out whether music purchases are offered for your Galaxy Tab.

In addition to using the Music Player app for listening to your MP3s, you might also find the Slacker app installed on your Galaxy Tab. (If you don't, download it for free from the Android Market.)

The Slacker app gives you online access to music via Slacker Personal Radio; think of it as an online radio station. It requires a Wi-Fi or 3G data connection, however. (You're listening to streaming music from the Web, so an Internet connection is absolutely required.)

FIGURE 9.7   Your music is listed on the Songs tab.

FIGURE 9.8   Music controls appear on screen as the song plays.

FIGURE 9.9 Your Galaxy Tab might offer a music service such as Rhapsody.

You are provided a long list of categories: Rock, Classic, and more. Just click a category, find a station, and tap it. Figure 9.10 shows how an online radio station opens, providing you with an album cover, band and song name, and some controls at the bottom that enable you to jump to the next song, mark a song as a favorite, and a button to ban a song or artist from ever playing again on your Galaxy Tab (using the Slacker app, of course).

Watching Videos

You can read books and listen to music with your Galaxy Tab, but what about watching videos? With the Galaxy Tab, you have many options (using Android Market apps), but two are immediately available to you: YouTube and Media Hub. YouTube is the most popular website for viewing uploaded video content provided by users and Media Hub enables you to preview, rent, or purchase feature films.

First, the Galaxy Tab comes with the YouTube app preinstalled. Figure 9.11 shows the opening screen after you tap the **YouTube** app.

FIGURE 9.10   Slacker Radio gives access to millions of songs.

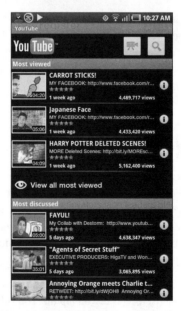

FIGURE 9.11   YouTube videos are listed using categories.

The YouTube app offers videos by dividing them into Most Viewed, Most Discussed, and Top Rated. Scroll down the list and simply tap a video to view it. But you can easily search for videos of interest by using the built-in Search feature at the top of the screen.

Tap a video, and it displays as shown in Figure 9.12. Videos play in Widescreen mode, so rotate your Galaxy Tab to watch your selected video. Tap the screen to see controls (such as pause) and a drag bar that you can use to move forward and backward through a video.

Tap the **Menu** button to see a Details button that provides more information about the video (such as its rating and number of views) and a Rating button for you to give the video a one- to five-star rating. You can also use the **Share** button to email a link of the video to friends.

FIGURE 9.12 Watch your video in Widescreen mode.

The other option for watching videos is the Media Hub app. When you launch it, you see a screen similar to the one in Figure 9.13.

You can tap the **Movie Store** option to view a library of movies available for rent or purchase as seen in Figure 9.14. Tapping a movie provides a summary, including run time and rating, plus an Own button (to buy) and a Rent button. (Be aware that some movies do not offer the option to rent.)

FIGURE 9.13   Use Media Hub to watch movies.

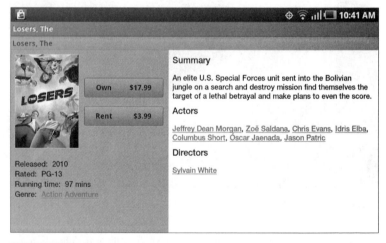

FIGURE 9.14   Rent or purchase a movie to download it to the Galaxy Tab.

You have to create a Media Hub account to purchase or rent from the store, but after you do, you can download movies to your Galaxy Tab for watching in the Media Hub app.

Summary

In this lesson, you were shown how to purchase and read books and magazines with the Kindle app, how to listen to music with either the Music Player app or with the Slacker Radio app, and how to watch videos via YouTube or the Media Hub.

Helpful Tips and Useful App Suggestions

In this lesson, you learn how to make your Galaxy Tab even more useful with additional apps. You also learn about online Galaxy Tab communities that can provide help, advice, and app reviews.

Monitoring Battery Life

The Galaxy Tab has a great battery that can provide many hours of useful service, but playing games, enabling Wi-Fi and GPS, and taking photos and videos take their toll. The Galaxy Tab alerts you when the battery dips below 20% by popping up an alert on screen that reminds you to plug in your charger.

The battery icon in the upper-right corner of the screen doesn't provide you with an exact percentage, so if you want to know exactly how much battery power you have left, tap the **Menu** button and select the **Settings** option. From the scrollable list, select **About Device**, and then click the **Status** category. You see a screen that provides you with the battery level percentage, like the one in Figure 10.1.

Checking for Updates

Android operating system updates are released periodically, and the best way to check for them is to visit the Settings options (tap the **Menu** button while viewing a home page). Scroll down the list and choose **About Device** and tap the **System Updates** category. If an update exists, tap it and follow the instructions to update your Galaxy Tab.

FIGURE 10.1   Knowing the battery level percentage is useful.

Learning to Use the Keyboard

If you've been using the Galaxy Tab's built-in onscreen keyboard, you might not be taking advantage of some of the keyboard shortcuts available. The Galaxy Tab supports a keyboard function called Swype that enables you to type words without lifting your finger from the onscreen keyboard.

To get some training in Swype, open the Settings screen and tap the **About Device** option. Next, tap the **System Tutorial** category and follow along as the short tutorial shows you a faster method for using the onscreen keyboard. Figure 10.2 shows the Swype tutorial in progress. You can see in the figure how a solid line is used to trace the path of your finger as you spell a word.

FIGURE 10.2   Use the Swype tutorial for better keyboard usage.

Using the Task Manager

The Galaxy Tab can run multiple applications simultaneously, enabling you to move back and forth between apps without having to restart them and without losing data.

Sometimes, however, too many apps running can cause the Galaxy Tab to be a bit sluggish. You might also encounter the occasional app that locks up and refuses to close down or continue. When this happens, the Task Manager is a useful app that enables you to not only view all the apps currently open but also enables you to close down apps with a single touch.

You can find the Task Manager app in the Applications group. Open it and you see a screen like the one in Figure 10.3. You can close any apps, misbehaving or otherwise, by just tapping the **End** button beside the name of the app you want to close.

FIGURE 10.3   Close down apps using the Task Manager.

Using Online Help

The Galaxy Tab might be a new device, but you won't have to worry about finding online help when you have problems or questions.

First, the Galaxy Tab runs the Android operating system—the same operating system found on many mobile phones. Because it's the same OS, there's already a large amount of technical support articles and web discussion forums that focus just on the OS. A few websites dedicated to the Android OS include the following:

▶ **http://androidcommunity.com/** provides the latest news on the Android OS as well as one of the oldest discussion forums.

▶ **http://www.droidforums.net/forum/** focuses on everything Android, but you'll find a newly formed Galaxy Tab discussion area in the list.

▶ **http://androidforums.com** focuses more on Android for mobile phones, but you'll find a lot of helpful folks willing to answer questions about the Galaxy Tab because of its similarities to the Galaxy S mobile phone.

Although these forums are great for learning more about the Android OS, they're wide ranging in their coverage of various devices. For more specific forums dedicated to just the Galaxy Tab, you can check out these newly formed web discussion boards and join the discussions:

▶ **http://www.galaxytabforum.org/** is new, so don't expect a lot of material to sift through just yet. But the members on this board want the site to grow, so join them and help grow the knowledge base for the Galaxy Tab by offering up your own advice if you find a question you can answer.

▶ **http://www.thegalaxytabforum.com/** is another new website devoted to the Galaxy Tab. This one also has a section of the forum that focuses on carrier-specific Galaxy Tab questions.

TIP: **Don't Be a Newbie**

Most web forums have a FAQ (frequently asked question) link that provides rules and suggestions for using the site. Read it over; you can often find links to the most common problems (with solutions) and suggestions for not becoming a nuisance to other members. The last thing you want to do is post your first question and find out it's been asked 50 times already and been answered in the first FAQ posting that you skipped over.

Connecting to a Windows PC

You can always email yourself photos and videos that you've stored on your Galaxy Tab, but a faster way to transfer files (in both directions) is to connect your Galaxy Tab to your computer with the USB cable.

The first time you connect it, you should see a window that contains a few files. Tap the **Samsung_Mobile_USB_Driver.exe** file and follow the instructions. When the driver is installed, you see a screen like the one in Figure 10.4.

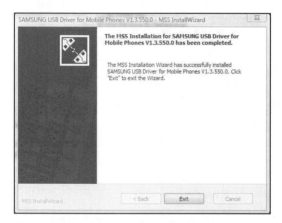

FIGURE 10.4   Install the driver if you want to transfer files.

Now, any time you connect the Galaxy Tab to your Windows PC, you see a screen appear on the Galaxy Tab like the one in Figure 10.5.

FIGURE 10.5   You must mount the Galaxy Tab to gain access to its storage.

When asked if you want to turn on USB Storage, tap the **Mount** button. On your Windows PC, you then see a screen like the one in Figure 10.6.

FIGURE 10.6   Read all app alerts before continuing with a download.

Tap the **Open Folder to View Files** option. You are then given access to the Galaxy Tab's storage. Figure 10.7 shows the file structure.

Photos and videos taken with your Galaxy Tab are stored in the DCIM folder under a subfolder titled Camera. Screenshots that you've taken are stored in the ScreenCapture folder. Any digital books or magazines that you've purchased with the Kindle app are in the Kindle folder.

Additional apps that you download and install might add their own folders to this structure. You might have to do some hunting to locate files you want to transfer or back up to your Windows PC. Likewise, you can easily transfer photos, videos, and other files to your Galaxy Tab by performing drag-and-drop actions or copy and pasting files from your PC to the Galaxy Tab.

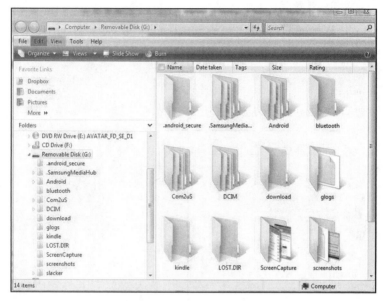

FIGURE 10.7   The file structure for the Galaxy Tab.

Interesting Apps

The rest of this lesson describes five suggested apps that both the author and tech editor have found useful or fun.

ShopSavvy

Okay, I absolutely love this app. Why? Because it enables me to take a snapshot of a product's bar code and then gives me a listing of local and online sources for purchasing the same item, often at a lower price.

Figure 10.8 shows how it works. You run the app and focus the camera on a bar code for a second or two. The line running down the center of the box in Figure 10.8 scans the bars and spaces of the bar code.

If the item can be identified (in Figure 10.8, I scanned the *Sams Teach Yourself Tumblr in 10 Minutes* book), the ShopSavvy app net supplies you with a listing of online and local businesses that sell the item. As you can

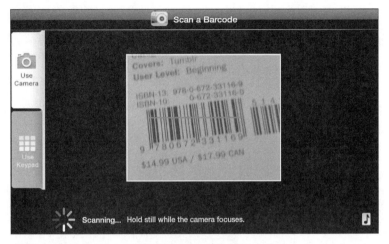

FIGURE 10.8 Scan a bar code of a product to find prices.

see in Figure 10.9, the app identified a source for the book at a low price of $7.99.

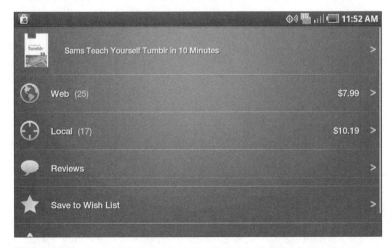

FIGURE 10.9 Use the item and location listing to find the best price.

TIP: **Remember the Shipping Costs**

Just because you can obtain an item online at a lower price does-n't mean it's cheaper. Often, shipping costs bump the price of an item up enough to make buying it locally a better option.

One thing ShopSavvy app developers recommend is to take your Galaxy Tab with you shopping. When you find an item you like, use ShopSavvy. If you find the same item at a nearby store for a lower price, you can immediately show the manager and try to negotiate for a price reduction or at least a price match.

This worked for me a few days ago at an electronics retailer when I found a piece of software (okay, a game) that I wanted for $24.95. I used ShopSavvy and found the same game at a store just 5 minutes away, for a price of $19.96. I asked the manager and he beat the price by $1. (He also asked me for a demo of the Galaxy Tab, which I was happy to provide.)

Dropbox

The Galaxy Tab is small enough to carry with you almost anywhere. Its portability, combined with the apps you have installed on it, means you always have access to your music, email, books, and other files.

But what about the files stored on your home or work computer? Wouldn't it be nice if you could access those files using your Galaxy Tab while you're away? With Dropbox, you now have a 100% free solution for mak-ing files available from any device that has an Internet connection.

Download and install the Dropbox app from the Android Store. The first time you run the app, you either have to provide your Dropbox user account info (if you're an existing Dropbox user) or create a new account. After you log in with your Dropbox account, you see a screen like the one in Figure 10.10. (Of course, your Dropbox might be empty; time to fill it!)

Figure 10.10 shows files that I can open and view on my Galaxy Tab. To gain access to these files, I installed the Dropbox software on my home computer and a Dropbox icon was placed on the desktop. After double-clicking that icon, the Dropbox folder opens and files I dragged into that folder now show up on my Galaxy Tab when I run the Dropbox app.

FIGURE 10.10   Use Dropbox to access files from anywhere.

One nice feature about Dropbox is that I can also log in at www.dropbox.com and access these files from a web browser. This means I have access to these files from my friends' computers, from a kiosk computer in the mall (that's running a web browser), or any other device that offers a web browser or supports a Dropbox app.

I can view JPEGs, PDFs, Word documents (if there is a Microsoft Office compatibility app on my Galaxy Tab—and there is one called ThinkFree Write), and even listen to MP3 songs stored in the Dropbox folder.

Astrid

I'm a checklist person; give me a list of things to do along with a little checkbox and I'm very productive. I cannot stand to leave a box unchecked and go to great lengths to check that box.

That's why I was very happy to find Astrid. It's a free app from the Android Market, and you can see the app in use in Figure 10.11.

FIGURE 10.11   Astrid is a to-do list for your Galaxy Tab.

Adding new tasks is easy from the Astrid app, but my favorite part is that I don't even have to access the app to add a new task. Take a look at Figure 10.12 and you see that I've added the Astrid app as a widget to my home screen. (See Lesson 2, "Configuration and Notifications," for steps on adding a widget.) The widget gives me a few of my current tasks, and I can click the widget to immediately add a new task.

Voice Recorder

There are many free voice recorder apps available, plus all the ones that cost you a few dollars. The one I've found and use that I like the best is the one by Mamoru Tokashiki. It has a simple interface and doesn't try to overwhelm you with bells and whistles.

FIGURE 10.12 The Astrid widget on my home screen.

Figure 10.13 shows the basic interface.

Not only can you save your recordings on the Galaxy Tab, but the app also enables you to email the recording (via Gmail) immediately after you click the **Stop** button. (It does use the .3gp file extension for saved files, so you need to download a 3GP player for your computer if you want to listen to the recordings.)

SnapMap

As I was writing this book, my technical editor, David Levy, was hard at work developing an app for the Android operating system. He's a programmer and thought it would be interesting to try his hand at creating an app for the Galaxy Tab (and any other device running Android).

As the book was nearing completion, he was sharing the app with me to test and provide feedback. It was a fun process, and something that I felt should be included in the book as not only an example of how fast apps can appear in the Android Market but also to demonstrate that there's an app for everything!

FIGURE 10.13   Voice Recorder is an easy-to-use recording app.

Figure 10.14 shows the basic feature of the SnapMap app; it enables you to drop "breadcrumbs" along your path as you travel, by car, train, or even foot. It's a fun way to share your adventures with friends and family, and the current features enable you to send your travel data to the web for viewing.

Future features (that are likely to be available when this book is released) include the capability to add notes, photos, and videos to document your journey. Because the app uses the GPS feature to track your path, every breadcrumb you drop contains time and location data. David's also hoping to enable users to share their SnapMap travels via Twitter and Facebook, so keep an eye out for this fun little app. I'm already using it with my three-year-old son to show him the path we take to school and the grand-parents' house. (He likes to press the button to drop the breadcrumbs.)

FIGURE 10.14   Drop breadcrumbs in SnapMap to track your journey.

Summary

In this lesson you were shown how to perform some additional tasks that can help make your Galaxy Tab more useful to you. You also learned about some of the online forums available for questions and information and some new apps that you might find useful/fun.

Index

SamsTeachYourself

from Sams Publishing

Sams **Teach Yourself in 10 Minutes**
offers straightforward, practical answers
for fast results.

These small books of 250 pages or less
offer tips that point out shortcuts and
solutions, cautions that help you avoid
common pitfalls, and notes that explain
additional concepts and provide additional
information. By working through the
10-minute lessons, you learn everything
you need to know quickly and easily!

When you only have time for the answers,
Sams Teach Yourself books are your
best solution.

Visit **informit.com/samsteachyourself**
for a complete listing of the products
available.

FREE Online Edition

Your purchase of **Sams Teach Yourself Samsung Galaxy Tab(tm) in 10 Minutes** includes access to a free online edition for 45 days through the Safari Books Online subscription service. Nearly every Sams book is available online through Safari Books Online, along with more than 5,000 other technical books and videos from publishers such as Addison-Wesley Professional, Cisco Press, Exam Cram, IBM Press, O'Reilly, Prentice Hall, and Que.

SAFARI BOOKS ONLINE allows you to search for a specific answer, cut and paste code, download chapters, and stay current with emerging technologies.

Activate your FREE Online Edition at www.informit.com/safarifree

> **STEP 1:** Enter the coupon code: HWSBIWH.

> **STEP 2:** New Safari users, complete the brief registration form. Safari subscribers, just log in.

If you have difficulty registering on Safari or accessing the online edition, please e-mail customer-service@safaribooksonline.com